CIVIL WAR SITES IN VIRGINIA

A Tour Guide

CIVIL WAR SITES
IN VIRGINIA
A Tour Guide

James I. Robertson Jr.
and Brian Steel Wills

REVISED EDITION

University of Virginia Press   Charlottesville and London

University of Virginia Press
© 2011 by the Rector and Visitors of the University of Virginia
Printed in the United States of America on acid-free paper

First published 2011

9 8 7 6 5 4 3 2 1

LIBRARY OF CONGRESS CATALOGING-IN-PUBLICATION DATA
Robertson, James I.
    Civil War sites in Virginia : a tour guide / James I. Robertson Jr. and Brian
Steel Wills.—Rev. ed.
        p. cm.
    Includes index.
    ISBN 978-0-8139-3111-1 (pbk. : alk. paper) — ISBN 978-0-8139-3130-2
(e-book)
        1. Virginia—History—Civil War, 1861–1865—Battlefields—Guidebooks.
2. United States—History—Civil War, 1861–1865—Battlefields—Guidebooks.
3. Battlefields—Virginia—Guidebooks. 4. Historic sites—Virginia—
Guidebooks. 5. Virginia—History—Civil War, 1861–1865. 6. Virginia—
Guidebooks. I. Wills, Brian Steel, 1959– II. Title.
    F224.3.R63 2011
    917.5504'44—dc22

                                                                    2010035065

Title page art: Henry Hill, Manassas National Battlefield Park. (Photograph by
Bettina Woolbright)

Illustration credits follow the index.
Maps by Chris Harrison.

Contents

Preface

No state contributed more to the Southern Confederacy, or suffered more from the Civil War, than did Virginia. The Old Dominion had traditionally been a leader of the American experiment in democracy. Beginning as a haven of patriots, Virginia became a producer of presidents. Its statesmen held front-rank positions in every decade during the United States' first half-century. Virginia possessed a prestige that the embryonic Southern nation sorely needed.

Prestige was only a part of what Virginia had to offer. Its borders stretched from the Atlantic Ocean to the Ohio River. Washington, D.C., the national capital, was literally a next-door neighbor. Over 1,047,000 residents made Virginia the most populous of Southern states. Its resources included a rich diversity of mineral deposits, harbors, farmlands, and livestock. Virginia's capital, Richmond, was the most industrialized city south of Philadelphia. The Confederate States of America would not have lasted four years had not Virginia given so much of itself to the Southern cause.

The Old Dominion was one of the last states to leave the Union. Yet because it was the most exposed geographically of the seceding states, Virginia became the major battleground of the Civil War. The bitterest and bloodiest fighting in the history of the Western Hemisphere took place in a narrow band of land extending from Manassas to Petersburg. Thousands of Americans were killed, and tens of thousands more were wounded or captured, as fields and woods became sanctified by the blood of Northerners and Southerners who were tragically fighting for the same thing. America, as each side interpreted what the American nation should be.

That the Confederacy survived during 1861–65, that the war raged without resolution for four long years, was attributed in large measure to the military leadership furnished by Virginia. Any list of generals begins almost invariably with Robert E. Lee. As commander of the Army of Northern Virginia, he had responsibility for the defense of most of the state. Lee proved to be a veritable genius at strategic maneuver as he shifted attention away from the Southern capital at Richmond. Not until two years after Lee assumed command—in 1864, when Confederate forces were in a state of irreversible deterioration—was a Federal army able to advance any distance south of the Rapidan River.

By April 1865, however, Virginia lay prostrate. It had borne more combat and absorbed more bloodshed than any other single state. Twenty-six major battles, more than 400 smaller engagements, plus the years of maneuvering by opposing armies, had wrought widespread destruction. Northern Virginia lay in ruins. The Shenandoah Valley had been systematically destroyed. Much of Fredericksburg and Richmond were in ashes. Petersburg was pockmarked from bombardments. Norfolk and the Hampton Roads naval works were in shambles. Countless farms and homes were charred skeletons of past splendor.

Then there was the human toll. Eighteen Virginia generals were among the more than 17,000 sons of the Old Dominion who had perished in battle or died from sickness. No way exists to measure the full impact of such a loss.

Virginia was also the only state in the Civil War to lose territory as a direct result of hostilities. A third of the Old Dominion broke away and, in 1865, became a separate state.

Today Virginia is vibrant, diverse, and progressive. It thinks of the present and plans for the future. Yet Virginia also remembers the past, more so perhaps than most states. To begin to forget, to fold away years gone by, Virginians first had to recall and pay tribute.

This the state has done to a commendable degree. Hundreds of monuments dot the land. The many preserved battlefields are quiet now, with only the wind disturbing areas where the blood of patriots merged. The graves of Civil War soldiers have the aura of shrines. In the 1930s Virginia became the first state in the nation to establish official highway historical markers, and the project continues still. Today more than 460 of those markers provide on-site information about Civil War events and participants.

Until now, no concerted effort has ever been made to catalog all of the major Civil War attractions in the Old Dominion. This book seeks to meet that need by providing data on and directions to every site of significance. Most of the monuments and markers were erected in the years before the construction of the interstate highway system. Visitors must therefore proceed on national and state roads when in quest of historical reminders.

In Virginia, the number of extant Civil War buildings is so high that certain restrictions had to be established for inclusion here. Buildings and homes which have been appreciably altered over the years so that they bear little resemblance to their wartime appearance have been omitted. Private homes, for the most part, are cited only when the current owners have expressed willingness to have visitors inspect the grounds. On the lawn of almost every county courthouse in the state is a monument of some kind to Confederate soldiers from that area. Included in this tour guide are only those of unique design and those bearing useful lists of names.

Many Civil War points of interest in Virginia are victims of time and nature. Fort Sedgwick, a key point in the 1864–65 siege of Petersburg, is now the site of an automobile service station. Where Libby Prison stood in Richmond is a parking lot. Rattlesnakes, bats, and lack of lighting make three wartime saltpeter mines in Wise County too dangerous to visit. On the other hand, here for the first time is a guide to scores of visitable Civil War attractions.

To organize the sites and facilitate tours, this book divides Virginia into six geographic sections. Descriptions of Civil War scenes in each section are code-numbered on maps to correspond with numbers affixed to each locale or site in the narrative. Each summary also contains specific directions for reaching that attraction via today's highways.

Unless otherwise noted, all sites mentioned here are free of charge.

Many of the scenes of yesteryear have a symbolism that reawakens a common patriotism. In a small cemetery at Appomattox, eighteen soldier-graves stand in a row. Seventeen of them contain Confederate soldiers; the grave at the end is that of a Federal soldier. They sleep side by side, and it is fitting that they do; for these American heroes who lived not so long ago struggled greatly against something greater than themselves. Often fighting for nothing more than the realization of a dream, they bravely marched down the undiscovered road to tomorrow. What they gave, we now share. What they lost, we gained. Their sacrifice is the nation's legacy.

I am genuinely grateful to scores of persons who responded in writing to inquiries about historic sites in every community of the state. Particularly I am indebted to the following friends who shared their love of Civil War history by giving me personal tours of scenes in their locales: Ernest C. Clark, Glade Spring; John E. Divine, Waterford; Robert C. Fries, Culpeper; Emory L. Hamilton, Wise; Kim Bernard Holien, Alexandria; Robert K. Krick, Fredericksburg; John V. Quarstein, Newport News; and Dabney W. Watts, Winchester.

The J. Ambler Johnston Research Fund of the VPI Educational Foundation made it possible for me to crisscross the state several times in order to examine historic sites. I shall always be inspired by "Uncle Ambler" Johnston and the lifelong love of Virginia that he possessed.

My wife Libba first pointed out the need for such a study. She gave me constant encouragement (as well as some prodding) throughout the various stages of compilation, and she was a valuable companion on research trips through the Old Dominion. In many ways, this is her book.

James I. Robertson Jr.
Virginia Polytechnic Institute and State University

Acknowledgments for the Revised Edition

Virginians and those who take an interest in the history of the great commonwealth, especially in the period of national turmoil of 1861–65, owe a debt of gratitude to James I. ("Bud") Robertson Jr., the renowned Civil War historian who generated this volume as a means of assisting those who wished to visit sites of importance to that conflict in Virginia.

Who better than Bud Robertson to take you on the paths of Robert E. Lee, Stonewall Jackson, and Jeb Stuart in the gray, or Ulysses Grant, Phil Sheridan, and George Custer in the blue? Bud has made an extraordinary contribution to Civil War literature through his scholarship. He offers another significant one here. As those of you who know him will readily affirm, Robertson has a nuanced understanding of the roles of the civilians and communities as well as the battles and leaders. The highlights of any tour include churches, cemeteries, and other public memorials, as well as the opportunity to walk the ground where Americans of both sides shed their blood and offered the most noble of sacrifices. All of Virginia's communities were touched in some manner by the introduction of war or the effects of war in their lives and those of the ones whom they held dear. Robertson takes the traveler along highways and byways that formerly resounded with the hooves of cavalry and the tramp of infantry. He allows the modern visitor to traverse fields where horrific carnage once marked the way, and lets us trace the steps of soldiers whose blood stained the floorboards of churches and homes that had been converted into hospitals to accommodate the wounded and dying.

Some of these sites have been lost to development, the passage of time, or other encroachments. Yet, many of those that still remain and are mentioned in this guide are the direct beneficiaries of increased interpretation and accessibility over the years since it first appeared. The number of state historic markers has increased significantly and the work of organizations such as the Shenandoah Valley Battlefield Foundation, the Central Virginia Battlefield Trust, the Richmond Battlefields Association, and myriad other parties interested in preserving and interpreting their portions of the saga have offered major contributions in preservation and interpretation of historically significant sites. National entities such as the Civil War Preservation Trust, formed by a merger in 1999 of the Association for the Preservation of Civil War Sites (1987) and the Civil War Trust (1991), have developed areas that were previously little-known or difficult to reach and understand. The Civil War Trails program has produced a comprehensive system of interpretive markers that have added immeasurably to the visitor experience. Taken together, all of the efforts of local communities and larger agencies, added to here by the often-poignant prose of one of Virginia's foremost authorities on the conflict, will only increase those opportunities. With the sesquicentennial of the American Civil War there may not be a better time to learn about and visit these sites than now.

I am grateful that Dick Holway offered me the opportunity to work with Bud on revising and updating this volume. The University of Virginia Press has made it possible to revisit these sites and provide additional information about them, and the new ones that have appeared since the original publication of this guide. Raennah Mitchell has been especially patient and helpful throughout this process. Thanks also goes to Mark Mones for his deft editing of the manuscript. I am also appreciative that my wife Elizabeth so readily offered her blessing and support for the project.

Thanks go to individuals associated with the Museum of the Confederacy, who saw the opportunity for enhancing the volume through modern photographic images. The woodcuts convey a sense of the world as contemporary audiences saw it in mid-nineteenth-century publications, while modern-day travelers will see these sites under different circumstances today. Indeed, the struggle to save sites associated with the conflict remains a vital and important part of ensuring that future generations will continue to be able to enjoy and learn from them.

Finally, Dr. Robertson and I have tried to make pursuit of the sites associated with the Late Unpleasantness in Virginia as pleasant as possible, but as Bud notes in his original preface, this book was Libba Robertson's. It remains a tribute to both her devotion to her husband and to his pursuit of the history whose love they also shared for so many years. I am pleased to be a part of the project and extend, along with Bud, the hope that you will use this guide to your make the most of your travel experiences throughout the Old Dominion.

Brian Steel Wills
Kennesaw State University, Georgia

CIVIL WAR SITES IN VIRGINIA

A Tour Guide

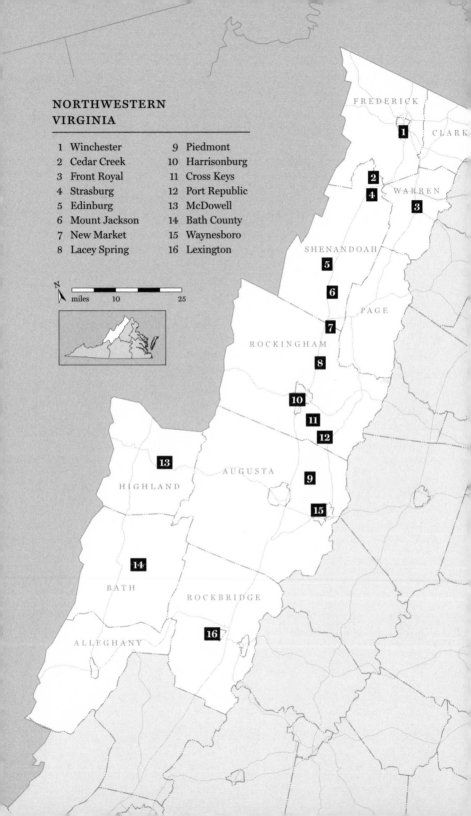

NORTHWESTERN VIRGINIA

N

miles   10   25

FREDERICK

CLARK

WARREN

SHENANDOAH

PAGE

ROCKINGHAM

HIGHLAND

AUGUSTA

BATH

ROCKBRIDGE

ALLEGHANY

NORTHWESTERN VIRGINIA

The Shenandoah Valley (also known as the Valley of Virginia) extends southwestward from the Potomac River to Lexington. Its fields and large orchards made it "the bread basket of the Confederacy," and the region was a principal source of supplies for Lee's Army of Northern Virginia during much of the war. In addition, the Valley was a veritable lifeline for both North and South. Lying between the two easternmost ranges of the Appalachian Mountains, leading northward as well as southward, it was also like a dagger pointed at the western flank of the Union and Confederate armies. Neither side could advance safely and far into enemy territory unless it had security in the Shenandoah Valley. This explains why the region was the scene of major campaigns in 1862 and again in 1864. All told, some 112 engagements of different types were fought within its narrow confines.

In the early 1960s the Virginia Civil War Commission erected ten pairs of "Circle Tour" markers at the sites of the major battles. The concept was to enable tourists to make a circular tour between Winchester and Harrisonburg via U.S. 11 and U.S. 340. These signs are excellent visual aids to the principal engagements in the Valley.

WINCHESTER   NW 1

Once called "the gateway to the Shenandoah Valley," Winchester was the most strategic point in the 135-mile Shenandoah corridor. As a result, it became the scene of more warfare than any other town west of Richmond. Winchester was reputed to have changed hands 72 times during the war as units of varying sizes and durations of time passed through its vicinity. It contained as many as six military hospitals. Commanding generals on both sides used it for a headquarters. By the war's end, the community was a battered shell of what it once had been.

MAJOR BATTLEFIELDS

Four major engagements were fought in and around the city: Kernstown (March 23, 1862), First Winchester (May 25, 1862), Second Winchester—or Stephenson's Depot (June 14–15, 1863), and Third Winchester—or Opequon Creek (September 19, 1864). Traces of these battlegrounds are now accessible for visitors. The Third Winchester battlefield has been expanded in interpretation and includes Fort Collier, the site of a September 19, 1864 assault by Union cavalry commander George Armstrong Custer.

In the 2100, 2700, and 3000 blocks of Valley Lane (U.S. 11 South)—all on the west side of the highway—are markers commemorating the 1862 battles. Circle Tour signs for Second and Third Winchester are located on the west side of U.S. 11 at the northern edge of town. Engagements in this region associated with the retreat of Jubal Early from his 1864 Maryland campaign against Washington, D.C., included Cool Spring (July 17–18, 1864), located east of Winchester and north of Virginia 7, and Second Kernstown (July 24, 1864).

Stonewall Jackson's headquarters, Winchester.

OLD COURT HOUSE CIVIL WAR MUSEUM

The Georgian-style court house building dating from 1840 saw many uses during the conflict, serving as a hospital, barracks, and prison. The walls carry some of the graffiti of soldiers from both sides who spent time there. Over 3,000 artifacts are available to visitors for viewing. Admission charge.

Located in the Loudoun Street Walking Mall in Old Town Winchester at 20 N. Loudoun Street.

CONFEDERATE MONUMENT

Dedicated in 1916 and restored in 1979, the memorial in front of the museum depicts in bronze a young Virginia infantryman departing for war.

JACKSON'S HEADQUARTERS

During November 1861–March 1862, Gen. Thomas J. ("Stonewall") Jackson had his headquarters in a French-style home that is now a museum. Many Jackson memorabilia are on display. Admission charge.

415 N. Braddock Street, one block west of the downtown's Loudoun Street Mall.

SHERIDAN'S HEADQUARTERS

Federal Gen. Philip H. Sheridan directed operations in the 1864 second Valley campaign from this imposing home. It was from here, on October 19, 1864, that Sheridan began his famous ride to rally the crumbling Union army under attack at Cedar Creek. Known as the Lloyd-Logan Home, the one-time Episcopal Female Institute and Elk's Club lodge is now the site of a local business.

A marker denotes an outline of the structure's significance and its connection to Union Gens. Robert Milroy and Nathaniel Banks as well as Sheridan.

135 N. Braddock Street, on the southwest corner of Braddock and Piccadilly streets.

STONEWALL CEMETERY

Some 3,000 identified Confederate soldiers are interred here. In addition, a tall stone shaft in the center of the cemetery honors 829 unknown Southern troops killed in the fighting around Winchester. The obelisk, dedicated in 1866, is among the earliest Civil War monuments. General Turner Ashby, Jackson's cavalry chief, is one of the notables buried here.

Boscawen Street runs east from downtown and leads into Mount Hebron Cemetery, of which the Confederate burial ground is a part.

NATIONAL CEMETERY

Here lie 2,110 known and 2,381 unknown Federals who died in the Winchester campaigns. This is one of the largest national cemeteries in Virginia.

Across Woodstock Lane from Stonewall Cemetery.

ENTRENCHMENTS

On U.S. 322 South, 3 miles from Winchester and on the north side of the highway, can be seen earthworks constructed in 1863 by Federals occupying the town. These remains are on private property.

SHAWNEE SPRINGS HOSPITAL

Established after the Third Battle of Winchester in the latter part of 1864, this temporary facility quickly became the largest of its type in the war. Dubbed Sheridan Field Hospital in honor of the commander whose medical director had sought its creation, the hospital processed thousands of Union troops, peaking in number from casualties produced at Cedar Creek. A Civil War Trails marker denotes the location of the field hospital.

Opequon Avenue in the Shawnee Springs Preserve.

CEDAR CREEK   NW 2

The last-ditch Confederate attempt here to dislodge Federals from the Valley was a dramatic battle of might-have-beens. At dawn on October 19, 1864, Gen. Jubal A. Early's Southern army delivered a heavy surprise attack that soon had two Federal corps on the verge of rout. Ragged and starving Confederates then began falling out of action in order to loot abandoned camps. Federal General Sheridan had just reached Winchester after a conference in Washington. Sheridan quickly mounted his horse, raced to the battlefield, and rallied his forces. "Affairs at times looked badly," he reported, "but by the gallantry of our brave officers and men, disaster has been converted into a splendid victory." Cedar Creek was the last major battle fought for

Sheridan's Ride, Battle of Cedar Creek, drawing by Alfred R. Waud, 1864.

control of the Shenandoah Valley. Today several highway markers pinpoint the battle site.

A half-mile south of Middletown alongside U.S. 11; take Exit 302 from I-81.

BELLE GROVE

This mansion, which was completed in 1794, is where James and Dolley Madison spent their honeymoon. In the autumn of 1864 Sheridan used the home as headquarters. It now houses a museum that is open during April–October. Admission charge.

Located in the center of the Cedar Creek battlefield.

FRONT ROYAL   NW 3

This seat of Warren County was chartered in 1788 and initially known as "Hell Town." The city became a base for Belle Boyd, a teenager who was an accomplished spy on behalf of Confederate efforts in the Valley. On May 23, 1862, Stonewall Jackson's men stormed the Union garrison here and captured 750 of 1,000 Federals.

WARREN RIFLES CONFEDERATE MUSEUM

Included in the displays are memorabilia relative to Miss Boyd, Lee, Jackson, Early, Ashby, and other Confederate leaders, plus artifacts of the war in the Valley. The museum is open from mid-April to November. Admission charge.

95 Chester Street in the downtown area.

SOLDIERS' CIRCLE MONUMENT

This memorial stands over the graves of 276 Confederate dead.

Located in Prospect Hill Cemetery.

MOSBY MONUMENT

This monument is flanked by two Parrott rifled cannon. The stone commemorates seven members of Mosby's Rangers who were illegally executed as spies by Federals at Front Royal in the autumn of 1864.

Located in Prospect Hill Cemetery.

BATTLE OF FRONT ROYAL MONUMENT

This bronze plaque atop a stone base summarizes the May 1862 engagement.

Intersection of Royal Avenue and Chester Street.

STRASBURG   NW 4

This village had strategic value during the war because of its location at the northern base of Massanutten Mountain, which divides the Shenandoah Valley in half for fifty miles. Signal Knob, on the northern face of Massanutten, was used by both armies to spot troop movements. It still dominates the eastern skyline.

FISHER'S HILL

On September 22, 1864, occurred a late-afternoon battle in which Sheridan's overwhelming numbers inflicted a second major defeat on the Confederates in three days. The Southern army lost 1,400 men. Among the dead was Col. A. S. ("Sandie") Pendleton, who had been one of Jackson's favorite officers.

Circle Tour signs denote the site of the battle 2 miles south of Strasburg on U.S. 11.

HUPP'S HILL

Remains of trenches thrown up by Federals in 1864 can be seen 1 mile north of Strasburg along the west side of U.S. 11.

EDINBURG   NW 5

For a month in 1862 this town was the base of operations for Gen. Turner Ashby's Southern cavalry. Some 28 skirmishes took place in the vicinity during that period. In October 1864 Federals began a systematic destruction of the Valley known as "The Burning." Sheridan ordered the grain mills at Edinburg set afire. When two young women of the town appealed tearfully to Sheridan to spare the mills because they were Edinburg's only livelihood, the general ordered the flames extinguished. The Edinburg Mill still stands today.

Exit 279 off I-81.

Engraving of Brig. Gen. Turner Ashby.

MOUNT JACKSON   NW 6

This was an important wartime locale because it was the western terminus of the Manassas Gap Railroad, one of only two lines connecting the Shenandoah Valley with the rest of Virginia. The bridge at the south end of town was burned by Federals in their retreat following the 1864 battle of New Market. Just north of downtown, on the west side of U.S. 11, is an obelisk marking the graves of 112 unknown Confederate soldiers.

Exit 273 off I-81.

NEW MARKET   NW 7

One of the most dramatic battles of the Civil War took place here. On May 15, 1864, a Federal army advancing to destroy the railroad at Staunton met a hodgepodge force of Confederates that included 257 teenage cadets from the Virginia Military Institute. The outnumbered Southerners attacked in a drizzly rain and, after severe fighting, overran the Union lines. Today one of the finest Civil War museums in the state is on this battlefield. Displays, dioramas, artifacts, movies, and a walking tour are some of the attractions. Admission charge. Circle Tour markers of this engagement are 1.1 miles north of New Market on U.S. 11. Two hundred yards north of those signs is a monument to a Pennsylvania regiment which suffered 45 percent casualties in that battle.

Take Exit 264 off I-81 onto 211 West, with an immediate right onto Route 305 (George Collins Parkway). The battlefield is essentially located on the west side of the interstate.

LACEY SPRING   NW 8

Some maps will denote this spot as Lincoln Spring, for it was here that the ancestors of Abraham Lincoln first settled. Immediately northwest of the present village, on an elevation a quarter-mile west of U.S. 11, is a cemetery containing many of the sixteenth president's forebears.

Between Exits 251 and 257 off I-81, on parallel U.S. 11.

PIEDMONT   NW 9

After the battle of New Market, Federal forces once again penetrated into the Shenandoah Valley. Confederate Gen. William E. "Grumble" Jones met these troops near this little village, but failed to prevent them from proceeding toward Staunton. In the fight, Jones perished while attempting to rally his troops. A marker erected by the United Daughters of the Confederacy marks the initial phase of the fighting, while a Civil War Trails marker denotes the final phase and provides overall context.

Virginia 608 north of New Hope.

HARRISONBURG   NW 10

Located at the southern tip of Massanutten Mountain, Harrisonburg had an additional military value as a vital road junction. Stonewall Jackson used the town as a rendezvous point several times during the 1862 Valley campaign.

ELECTRONIC MAP

A large electrified relief map, along with a 27-minute narration, provides an excellent overview of the 1862 battles for control of the Shenandoah. Admission charge.

Harrisonburg–Rockingham County Historical Society, 301 S. Main Street.

BATTLE OF HARRISONBURG

On June 6, 1862, two regiments of Confederates attacked a Federal regiment, and in the ensuing fight for control of Chestnut Hill, Gen. Turner Ashby was killed. Descriptive markers and a monument at the site of Ashby's death are at the field. A Civil War Trails marker can be found 0.2 miles north of Neff Avenue and reached from a new Turner Ashby Lane that replaces an earlier version no longer accessible.

From Exit 245 on I-81, proceed 0.5 miles southeastward on County 659. Turn left on County 1003 for 0.4 miles. The markers are on the right.

CROSS KEYS   NW 11

Here and at nearby Port Republic is where the 1862 Valley campaign ended. In the second week of June, Jackson found himself between two approaching Federal armies. The Confederate general divided his smaller force to meet the dual threat. Federals under Gen. John C. Fremont marched out of Harrisonburg and on June 8 attacked part of Jackson's waiting army under Gen. Richard S. Ewell. A furious Southern counterattack inflicted almost 700 losses on Fremont's forces before they abandoned the field. The countryside today remains basically as it looked at the time of the battle. A bronze tablet on the north side of County

659 identifies the battleground. In addition, a Circle Tour set of highway markers on Virginia 276 a few hundred yards south of County 659 graphically describes the action.

Take Exit 245 (County 659) from I-81 southeastward for 7.2 miles.

PORT REPUBLIC   NW 12

On the day following Cross Keys occurred the climactic engagement of the 1862 campaign. Confederates under the personal command of Jackson assailed converging Federals along the eastern bank of the Shenandoah River. The Southerners were eventually victorious, but at a heavier cost in men. The battlefield now is relatively unmarked by progress.

A walking tour of "The Coaling," the main defensive position on which the heaviest fighting occurred, is available.

From Exit 245 (County 659) off I-81, drive 11.5 miles southeastward to the intersection with U.S. 340. Turn left—north—on U.S. 340 for 1.1 miles to Circle Tour markers, situated at a spot where the entire Port Republic battleground is clearly visible. Inside the village of Port Republic is also a useful roadside battle map.

KEMPER HOUSE

Home of the Port Republic Museum, this structure is the site to which the mortal remains of Turner Ashby were brought after the colorful Confederate cavalryman fell in a rear-guard action on June 6, 1862. It is open only on Sunday afternoons through the months of April to October.

Intersection of Port Republic Road (Route 253) and Water Street.

McDOWELL   NW 13

On May 8, 1862, the second major battle of the Valley campaign exploded when Jackson arrived here seemingly from nowhere and confronted a Federal army advancing eastward through the mountains. Fighting lasted five hours. At midnight, the Federals used campfires to mask their retreat from the area. Today

Kemper House, home of the Port Republic Museum.

the hills constituting Jackson's right flank are conspicuous from the highway; while the battlefield itself is virtually intact, it is all on private property. Two roadside markers pay tribute to the engagement. Inside the village—0.9 miles west of the battleground—stands the McDowell Presbyterian Church, which was one of the buildings used as a hospital during and after the fighting.

At exit 285 on I-81, take U.S. 250 west through Staunton for 35.1 miles. The picturesque highway snakes over four mountain ranges. On the mountaintop at the Augusta–Highland county line are remnants of Confederate entrenchments dug in the first year of the war. An example of the ability of preservationist efforts to enjoy modern successes, the McDowell battlefield has a Civil War Preservation Trust interpretive trail. Civil War Trails markers offer access and information about the site, which is also part of the Shenandoah Valley Battlefields Historic District. The Highland Museum and Heritage Center, Fort Johnson, and Sitlington Hill highlight the story, although the latter requires a steep climb to appreciate from the point at which Stonewall Jackson's artillery blazed against the Federals in the fighting.

BATH COUNTY NW 14

Although at the remote western edge of the state, Bath County boasts several Civil War attractions. The area is best reached east-to-west by Virginia 39 and north-to-south by U.S. 220. This is mountainous country, where slow driving is imperative.

MILLBORO SPRINGS

Just south of this mountainous village, on the right-hand (west) side of County 633, are remains of entrenchments and gun emplacements. Their origins are unknown.

BATH ALUM SPRINGS

This was a favorite wartime resort for soldiers and civilians. Only a few trees remain to show where the shaded driveway existed. During the winters of 1861–62 and 1863–64, Confederate cavalry camped in the fields north of the highway.

6.5 miles west of Millboro Springs on Virginia 39.

WARM SPRINGS

This well-known spa was a focal point for this area of the state during the war. The Warm Springs Hotel (no longer standing) served as a hospital and headquarters for both sides. The wartime courthouse is now an inn. The wife and children of Gen. Robert E. Lee spent much of the war here. In the Ladies' Bath House is a chair especially made for the arthritically crippled Mrs. Lee.

6.5 miles west of Bath Alum Springs.

FLAG ROCK

This promontory was signal post used by Confederates and Federals alike during the conflict.

Proceed 3 miles east of Warm Springs on Virginia 39 to the top of Warm Springs Mountain. Flag Rock is visible to the south.

WAYNESBORO   NW 15

On March 2, 1865, Federal cavalry under Sheridan broke Early's Confederate lines here and captured most of the town's 1,000 defenders. This engagement was the last major contest fought for control of western Virginia.

HARMAN MONUMENT

This simple stone marker stands at the spot where Col. William H. Harman died in the battle of Waynesboro. Harman, a resident of Waynesboro, had served from 1851 to 1863 as commonwealth's attorney for the county.

The marker, as well a highway historical sign, are on U.S. 250, 0.1 miles west of the intersection with U.S. 340.

CONFEDERATE MONUMENT

In Riverview Cemetery is an obelisk honoring some of the Southern troops who died at Waynesboro. Names from four states are listed on the shaft.

The cemetery is located on U.S. 340 at the first stoplight south of the junction of U.S. 340 and U.S. 250.

LEXINGTON   NW 16

No town of its size in Virginia contains more historical attractions. Lexington was the home of wartime governor John Letcher. It is the site of Virginia Military Institute, the South's premier military academy. So wedded to the Southern cause were Lexington's citizens that the tiny community sent an artillery battery and an infantry company into the service.

The town is accessible via Exits 188, 191, and 195 off I-81.

JORDAN POINT PARK

On June 10, 1864, Federal troops confronted Confederate defenders here. Succeeding in driving them away from the cross-

Stonewall Jackson house in Lexington (*above*), Jackson statue by Moses Eze-kiel, overlooking the parade ground at the Virginia Military Institute (*below*).

ing, the Union soldiers entered Lexington and burned a substantial portion of the town, including VMI buildings.

From I-64, take Exit 55. Signs mark the park entrance ahead and to the right along the river, with ample parking available.

JACKSON HOME
The only residence that Stonewall Jackson ever owned served as his home during his 10-year tenure as a VMI professor. The

building has been restored and furnished to appear as it looked during Jackson's stay there in the 1850s. Admission charge.

8 E. Washington Street, one block east of Main Street and across the street from the county courthouse.

STONEWALL JACKSON CEMETERY

Here lie the remains of Jackson, members of his family, and a number of the town's leading statesmen and soldiers. Some 400 Confederate soldiers are said to be buried in the cemetery.

300 block of S. Main Street.

WASHINGTON AND LEE UNIVERSITY

Robert E. Lee served as the college's president in the five years immediately after the Civil War. The center of attraction on the campus is the Lee Memorial Chapel. The remains of Lee and most of his family are entombed here. Edward Valentine's recumbent statue of Lee is itself worth the trip to Lexington. In the basement of the chapel is a museum of college mementos, with emphasis on Lee's contributions.

Proceed one block west of Main Street on Henry Street to the visitor parking lot beside the chapel.

VIRGINIA MILITARY INSTITUTE

Since its establishment in 1839, this school has been one of the leading military academies in the Western Hemisphere. It contributed a host of officers and men to the Confederate cause. In the center of the campus is an unusual statue depicting Stonewall Jackson standing in the wind. Nearby are original cannon from the famous Rockbridge Artillery. On the east side of the parade ground stands Sir Moses Ezekiel's seated statue of *Virginia Mourning Her Dead,* a monument to the cadets who fell in the 1864 battle of New Market. An on-campus museum provides an excellent summary of VMI's heritage.

North of and adjacent to Washington and Lee University; North Main Street passes to the east of the parade ground.

NORTH CENTRAL VIRGINIA

1 Leesburg
2 Waterford
3 Aldie
4 Thoroughfare Gap
5 Warrenton
6 Little Fork Church
7 Kelly's Ford
8 Brandy Station
9 Culpeper
10 Cedar Mountain
11 Clark Mountain
12 Germanna Ford
13 Orange
14 Gordonsville
15 Charlottesville
16 Trevilian Station
17 Goochland County

NORTH CENTRAL VIRGINIA

The Piedmont region of Virginia lies between the flat coastal lands to the east and imposing mountains to the west. It is an area composed of gently rolling hills, small clumps of trees, and beautiful vistas. In 1860 fences of stone and rail were dividers between orchards, grainfields, and vast pasture lands. Communities were small and scattered, thereby making communication tenuous at best. The northern Piedmont thus became ideal for cavalry operations, and in the last two years of the war, a Virginia horseman so dominated activities in the region that it was often called "Mosby's Confederacy."

No area of the state suffered more in the Civil War than did north central Virginia. Scores of small engagements, streams of wounded men, hordes of stragglers from both armies, destruction of crops, and looting of homes were regular scourges. Little clothing, less food, no medicines, and sleepless concern over loved ones serving in Lee's army were other tribulations suffered by residents of this area. They felt the angry hand of the Civil War for almost the entirety of its four years. The occupations and counteroccupations by opposing armies ultimately gave the section another name: "The Desolate Land."

LEESBURG   NC 1

This was a focal point in northern Virginia for both armies. Lee shook down his forces here in September 1862 before launching the first invasion of the North. General Lewis A. Armistead of Gettysburg fame served as provost marshal of Leesburg for a time. The town is also associated with the exploits of Col. John S. Mosby, the legendary "Gray Ghost of the Confederacy." A number of wartime homes remain standing, but all are privately owned.

Retreat of the Federalists after the Fight at Ball's Bluff, from *The Illustrated London News,* 1861.

LOUDOUN MUSEUM

This small depository is in a vintage-1850s building and displays a number of Civil War artifacts.

16 W. Loudoun Street.

BALL'S BLUFF

Here occurred one of the first Union disasters of the war. When a Federal force of 1,000 men crossed the Potomac River on an October 1861 reconnaissance, Southern reinforcements rushed to the threatened area and drove the bluecoats back over the bluffs to the river's edge. Scores of Billy Yanks died from musketry from above; others drowned, their bodies floating slowly downriver to Washington. A small but impressive national cemetery and stone markers to two heroes in the fighting are on the battlefield today. There are numerous markers that provide context and interpretation located along the walking trail, all of which is incorporated in the Ball's Bluff Battlefield Regional Park.

From Virginia 7 at Leesburg, go north on U.S. 15 Bypass for 1.9 miles. Turn right on Ball's Bluff Road for 1 mile to the battle site.

WATERFORD   NC 2

In the center of this history-filled village is the Waterford Baptist Church, scene of shoot-out more characteristic of the American West. On August 27, 1862, a company of Federal cavalry took cover in the church when confronted by an equal number of Confederate troopers. The ensuing gun battle left the front of the brick structure pockmarked with bullets, which are quite visible still.

Waterford is 4 miles west of Leesburg via County 662. The church is at the intersection of County 665 and 783.

ALDIE   NC 3

Aldie, Middleburg, and Upperville were witness to bitter mounted engagements during June 17–21, 1863. Total losses were higher than those incurred subsequently by cavalry at Gettysburg. George A. Custer, William W. Averell, and Elon J. Farnsworth were all Federal junior officers in these engagements; yet a week later, all three had been elevated to the rank of brigadier general. The only memento of the three battles is a monument to the 1st Massachusetts Cavalry. One of its captains, Charles Francis Adams Jr., wrote of Aldie: "My poor men were just slaughtered and all we could do was stand still and be shot down."

From U.S. 50 at Aldie, turn north on County 734 for 1.3 miles to the monument at the top of the hill.

THOROUGHFARE GAP   NC 4

One of the major passes through the Blue Ridge Mountains, this area was of vital importance to both sides. The Confederate troops of Gens. Stonewall Jackson and James Longstreet used this pass in flanking movements that produced a smashing victory in the August 1862 battle of Second Manassas.

6.8 miles west of the intersection of Virginia 55 and U.S. 29.

This city was under Federal control for most of the war. It was the target of several raids by Mosby's partisan rangers. All but two of the town's churches were used as hospitals. Saint James Episcopal Church was left unharmed so that one place for worship by all denominations would be available. On the other hand, the Presbyterian church was converted into a stable. Warrenton contributed three companies to the Confederate armies. The most noted of those units was the "Black Horse Cavalry."

OLD COURT HOUSE

The present building, constructed after a fire in the 1890s, is an almost exact replica of the wartime courthouse. Among the portraits gracing the walls inside are likenesses of several Civil War figures from Fauquier County. A monument to Mosby stands on the courthouse lawn.

Located at the downtown crossroads where Warrenton began.

WARREN GREEN HOTEL

This was a commodious nineteenth-century hostelry. From the upper porch, in November 1862, Gen. George B. McClellan delivered his farewell address to the Federal Army of the Potomac that he had created. The building now houses county offices.

Across the street from the site is the "California Building," the law office and residence of Confederate general and Virginia governor William "Extra Billy" Smith.

Hotel Street in downtown Warrenton.

MOSBY HOME

Built around 1850, Brentmoor is an Italianate villa–style home and one of the most beautiful houses in the city. It became the postwar residence first of Col. Mosby and then of Gen. Eppa Hunton, who commanded a brigade in Pickett's Charge at Gettysburg. The home is the now site of the Mosby Museum. The Warrenton-Fauquier Visitor Center is adjacent to the home.

173 Main Street.

MARR HOUSE

This clapboard dwelling, also in private possession, was the residence of Capt. John Q. Marr of the "Warrenton Rifles." Killed in action on June 1, 1861, Marr is regarded as the first Civil War battle fatality in Virginia.

118 Culpeper Street.

WARRENTON CEMETERY

A tall shaft dominates this burial ground and marks the resting place of Col. John S. Mosby. Some 600 unknown Confederate soldiers are interred here.

Located on Lee Street, within walking distance of the downtown.

Col. John S. Mosby.

LITTLE FORK CHURCH NC 6

At this Episcopal church Company D ("The Little Fork Rangers") of the 4th Virginia Cavalry Regiment was organized. The troopers used the church grounds as a drill field before departing for war. A unique stone monument to this company stands behind the church.

Located midway between Warrenton and Culpeper, reached via Virginia 229 and County 624.

KELLY'S FORD NC 7

Only two markers call attention to the March 17, 1863, fight here. Opposing cavalry brigades fought a running battle over brush-covered terrain. One of those killed in the action was the youthful but inspiring Maj. John Pelham, who commanded Stuart's Horse Artillery. Three months earlier at Fredericksburg, Lee had praised the Alabamian as "the gallant Pelham."

Just south of the Rappahannock River crossing of U.S. 15-29 is Elkwood. In the front yard of a home at the intersection with County 685 is a weather-beaten monument to Pelham's memory. A few yards north of this intersection is the junction of U.S. 15-29 with eastbound County 674. Approximately 4 miles down the county road is Kelly's Ford itself. Deep in the woods (a path now exists) is a tiny marker supposedly pinpointing the spot where Pelham was leading men forward when he was struck by a shell fragment. Some historians dispute this site.

BRANDY STATION   NC 8

Often termed "the greatest cavalry battle ever fought on American soil," this June 9, 1863, engagement raged for 11 hours and extended over fields and through woods. The Confederates managed to retain the field; but in almost all other respects, the battle was a victory for Federal horsemen—their first major success

Cavalry Charge near Brandy Station, drawing by Edwin Forbes, 1864.

of the war. The battlefield today is virtually unchanged from its 1863 appearance. Two historical markers grace Fleetwood Hill, the key point in the fighting.

The headquarters for the interpretation of the fighting here and the Brandy Station Foundation can be found in the Graffiti House, a structure renowned for containing the scribblings of soldiers who passed through. Open on weekends.

Located 2.1 miles south of Elkwood on U.S. 15-29 and 5 miles north of Culpeper. At the junction with County 663, turn west to ascend Fleetwood Hill; the battlefield is visible a few hundred yards from the main highway. To reach Graffiti House, turn south on Alanthus Road and travel 200 yards to Brandy Road. Turn left.

CULPEPER   NC 9

The town of Culpeper was one of the most important points in Civil War Virginia. It was a railhead on the Orange and Alexandria Railroad; Robert E. Lee's army used it repeatedly for bivouac and encampment; Federal Gen. Ulysses S. Grant commandeered the hotel for his headquarters before the 1864 campaign; and many of the town's churches, homes, and commercial buildings became hospitals for soldiers wounded in nearby battles.

CULPEPER HISTORY MUSEUM

An earlier incarnation as the Culpeper Cavalry Museum, the complex has expanded its hours to include weekends. This small but impressive exhibit includes a 30-minute slide program on Culpeper's role in the war. The presentation fully explains why the city is sometimes called the "Cavalry Capital of the Civil War."

803 S. Main Street.

NATIONAL CEMETERY

The majority of Union soldiers in this rather large burial plot succumbed to illnesses such as pneumonia and typhoid fever.

From the downtown area, proceed 3 blocks east of Main Street to the cemetery entrance.

FAIRVIEW CEMETERY

In this principal cemetery for Culpeper stands a monument to a mass grave of Confederates, most of whom are unknown.

5 blocks west of Main Street on U.S. 522.

REDWOOD

John Strother Pendleton, one of Culpeper County's most influential wartime citizens, lived in this imposing mansion. Generals Lee and Longstreet met several times at Redwood; Gen. Jeb Stuart was a houseguest there; and it is believed that Maj. Pelham spent the night there before his death the following day at Kelly's Ford. The estate is privately owned, but the grounds may be visited.

From Main Street in Culpeper, take U.S. 522 (Sperryville Pike) for 1.2 miles. Turn left at the sign on the south side of the highway.

CEDAR MOUNTAIN   NC 10

On August 9, 1862, in rolling country south of Culpeper, Confederates under Stonewall Jackson collided with the van of Gen. John Pope's advancing Union army. Federal regiments attacked on both sides of the highway. Jackson's line barely held until reinforcements arrived and turned the tide of battle in the South's favor. The area today is as close to its wartime appearance as any battlefield in Virginia; a state highway marker denotes the battle site.

5.1 miles south of Culpeper on U.S. 15.

CLARK MOUNTAIN   NC 11

Here was a vital signal station for Confederate armies for much of the war. From its heights Jackson and Lee both observed Pope's movements before the Second Manassas campaign. On May 2, 1864, Lee stood atop the mountain and watched the beginning of Grant's advance into the Wilderness. The eminence still offers one of the most panoramic views of the Virginia Piedmont.

Travel south on U.S. 522 from Culpeper; the mountain will become increasingly conspicuous on the west side of the road. Just after crossing the Rapidan River, turn right (west) on a paved road marked by a Moormont Orchards sign. The road curls up to the mountaintop.

GERMANNA FORD   NC 12

This site was a heavily used crossing of the oftentimes imposing Rapidan River. Three times during the war (April 30 and November 16, 1863, and May 4, 1864) the Federal Army of the Potomac waded over the river here to launch offensives against Lee's forces.

Virginia 3 crosses the Rapidan precisely at Germanna Ford.

ORANGE   NC 13

Although this county seat was never witness to a major engagement, a number of skirmishes occurred near it. The town became a favorite rendezvous point for the Confederate Army of Northern Virginia.

COURTHOUSE

Architecturally, the courthouse looks as it did in wartime. Local units used the basement of the building for an arsenal in the conflict's first weeks.

Located in the center of town, on U.S. 15.

SAINT THOMAS'S EPISCOPAL CHURCH

This is the only surviving church in the area that reflects Thomas Jefferson's architectural tastes. In 1863 President Jefferson Davis, as well as Gens. Lee, A. P. Hill, William N. Pendleton, and other army notables, all attended services here. The pew where

Davis and Lee prayed is marked. According to local legend, Lee hitched his horse, Traveller, to a locust tree while attending services. One still stands in front of the church at that spot.

U.S. 15 ascends a hill just south of downtown Orange. Saint Thomas's is on the crest, a half-block south of the point where U.S. 15 makes a ninety-degree turn.

GORDONSVILLE   NC 14

The junction here of the Virginia Central and the Orange and Alexandria railroads made this village one of the strategically vital areas in north central Virginia. Gordonsville became a major supply depot; Confederate forces encamped here regularly; one of Virginia's larger military hospitals operated here for the last three years of the conflict.

THE CIVIL WAR MUSEUM AT THE EXCHANGE HOTEL

Originally constructed as an overnight accommodation for railroad travelers, this three-story building became the central structure for the Gordonsville Receiving Hospital. Ministering to over 70,000 soldiers from both sides throughout the conflict,

The Civil War Museum at the Exchange Hotel, Gordonsville.

the facility also served as a hospital for the Freedmen's Bureau after the war. Admission charge.

U.S. 33 at the eastern edge of the downtown area.

PRESBYTERIAN CHURCH

The church's beginnings go back to the 1840s. The sanctuary maintains its wartime appearance. One of the most beloved of Confederate ministers, Daniel B. Ewing, was pastor of the church. A plaque notes that Gen. Stonewall Jackson worshiped here several times in 1862.

U.S. 33 between the downtown and the traffic circle junction with U.S. 15.

MAPLEWOOD CEMETERY

Nearly 700 Confederate soldiers died at the receiving hospital. Temporarily buried behind the Exchange Hotel, the bodies were later reinterred in the local cemetery. Headstones were not placed over the individual graves. Today the remains lie in a grassy plot surrounded on three sides by woods, with a bronze marker denoting the burial ground.

From the traffic circle of U.S. 15 and 33, continue west on U.S. 33 for 0.6 miles. Turn right into the cemetery, continue straight until the semipaved road makes a ninety-degree curve to the left. Proceed another 20 yards. The plot and marker are on the right.

CHARLOTTESVILLE   NC 15

This city was known during the war primarily for its military hospitals. Federal troops seized and occupied Charlottesville in 1864.

UNIVERSITY CEMETERY

The remains of 1,200 Confederate soldiers, most of whom perished from sickness, lie here. Centerpiece of this burial ground is a bronze statue of a bareheaded Confederate soldier.

Northeast corner of Alderman and McCormick roads, just north of the University of Virginia football stadium.

LEE STATUE

Completed in 1924, this equestrian statue was the work of sculptors H. M. Shrady (who died while the project was underway) and Leo Lentelli.

Located in a small park 2 blocks north of the Downtown Mall, between 1st and 2nd streets.

JACKSON STATUE

This most impressive monument was the creation of Charles Keck and antedates the Lee statue by three years. The Jackson memorial is unique in that it depicts the general bareheaded, and galloping forward on his beloved mount, Little Sorrel.

3 blocks north of the Downtown Mall, on 4th Street.

TREVILIAN STATION   NC 16

Cavalry under Sheridan were moving westward in an attempt to establish a link between Grant's army at Richmond and Federal forces at Charlottesville. On June 11, 1864, troopers under George A. Custer attacked the Confederates of Wade Hampton and Fitzhugh Lee. The fighting was confused and indecisive. The following day, Sheridan renewed the assaults without success. In the two-day engagement, combined losses exceeded 1,700 men. Today a bronze plaque (dedicated by the United Daughters of the Confederacy) and a highway historical tablet call attention to the site of the first day's action. A Trevilian Station Battlefield driving tour and a number of Civil War Trails markers will assist you when touring these locations. Efforts have also been undertaken to preserve land through the Trevilian Station Battlefield Foundation.

The plaque and historical marker are 200 yards east of the junction of U.S. 33 and Virginia 22, on the south side of the highway.

GOOCHLAND COUNTY NC 17

GOOCHLAND COUNTY JAIL

This building, erected in 1825, served as a Federal prison in the latter part of the Civil War. In March 1865 Union cavalrymen liberated the inmates, then burned the building. Legend has it that a Pennsylvania captain prevented his men from setting fire to the nearby courthouse as well because he thought that the deeds needed to be preserved to prove ownership of land.

Located on Virginia 6 in the county seat of Goochland.

DOVER STEAM MILL RUINS

During the war this grinding mill was a two-story structure with arched voids. On March 1, 1864, Federal raiders under Col. Ulric Dahlgren burned the mill. Ruins of the mill are on private property.

From Virginia 6, proceed north on County 642 for 0.2 miles.

PLEASANTS MONUMENT

A stone marker honors James Pleasants, a county Confederate hero who reputedly captured 13 Federals and killed another.

From Goochland, drive west on Virginia 6 to County 670; turn right to the intersection with County 641 to reach the monument.

NORTHEASTERN VIRGINIA

1 Alexandria
2 Arlington
3 Fairfax County
4 Dumfries
5 Manassas
6 Stratford Hall
7 Fredericksburg
8 Chancellorsville-
Wilderness
9 Spotsylvania
10 Massaponax Church
11 Guinea Station
12 Carmel Church
13 Garrett Farm
14 North Anna
Battlefield

FAIRFAX

PRINCE
WILLIAM

STAFFORD

KING
GEORGE

SPOTSYLVANIA

WESTMORELAND

CAROLINE

RICHMOND

NORTHUMBER-
LAND

ESSEX

LANCASTER

N
miles   10   25

NORTHEASTERN VIRGINIA

On a map it looked so easy. The two opposing capitals, Richmond and Washington, lay only 110 miles apart. All the numerically superior Federal armies seemingly had to do was to lunge forward across the Potomac and make a four-day march southward. Seize Richmond and the South's political core—as well as its leading industrial city—would be lost and the war would be over. Yet Confederate military leaders were optimistically aware that a southward advance on Richmond would be costly for any invader. If Confederate shore batteries or naval vessels could keep Union gunboats out of Virginia's large rivers, and if Southern troops could control the few mountain passes through the Blue Ridge, the distance and terrain between the capitals offered the South an almost ideal defense.

Dense forests, broad rivers running west-to-east, and swampy areas were natural barriers to any move on Richmond from the north. Further impeding a Union advance was the vital rail junction of Manassas. Any movement from Washington had first to be southwest to the junction so as to protect the Union flank, then southeast toward Richmond. An expeditious Confederate general might choose his battleground and strike at any point in the narrow 100-mile-wide corridor between the mountains and the Chesapeake Bay. As long as the opposing armies bore any relation to each other in size, the Northern battle cry of "On to Richmond!" could be a siren's song, lulling Federal brigades onto a killing ground.

And a killing ground northeastern Virginia tragically became.

ALEXANDRIA   NE 1

This important river port was situated directly across the Potomac from the Northern capital. Hence, Alexandria became vulnerable from the moment of Virginia's secession from the Union.

The city dispatched four companies into Confederate service before its May 1861 occupation. Being safe behind the lines for the remainder of the war enabled Alexandria to escape destruction. Yet its use as a Federal supply base, hospital depot, and port of embarkation drastically altered its prewar appearance.

FORT WARD

One of the 68 forts and batteries that formed a defensive circle around Washington, Fort Ward stood on a commanding eminence and boasted 36 gun emplacements. The northwest bastion of the fort has been reconstructed, with renovations made to other portions of the works. The headquarters building contains numerous artifacts and displays. In many respects, this is the most attractive Civil War site in the greater Washington area. There is no admission charge, but donations are welcome.

Located at 4301 W. Braddock Road, which lies between Virginia 7 and Seminary Road west of downtown Alexandria.

IVY HILL CEMETERY

Here can be seen the graves of Frank Stringfellow, a noted scout for Gen. Jeb Stuart, and C.S. Navy Capt. Sidney Smith Lee.

From Fort Ward, proceed 1.7 miles east on King Street (Virginia 7); the cemetery is on the north side of the highway.

ALEXANDRIA NATIONAL CEMETERY

First begun in 1862, this burial ground contains the bodies of more than 3,750 Union soldiers. Also to be found here are the graves of four civilians, who assisted in—and died during—the pursuit of Lincoln assassin John Wilkes Booth.

Located at Wilkes and Payne streets in the downtown area.

FREEDMEN'S CEMETERY

Established in January 1864 on land confiscated from pro-Confederate Francis L. Smith, this ground became the final resting place for some 1,800 individuals, mostly African American refugees who had perished from disease. Although operating under the auspices of the Bureau of Refugees, Freedmen and

Abandoned Lands for a time after the war, it closed to further interments in 1869. Work on establishing the parameters of the cemetery continues with the view of putting into place a memorial park. A state marker was erected on the site in 2000.

Located at South Washington and Church Streets in Alexandria.

FREEDOM HOUSE MUSEUM

Located in the building that once housed a prominent Alexandria slave-mart, this museum is dedicated to the story of the individuals who endured the South's "peculiar institution." The Northern Virginia Urban League purchased the historic building and opened it to visitors in its new incarnation on February 12, 2008; guided tours are available on request.

1315 Duke Street.

17TH VIRGINIA INFANTRY MONUMENT

Most of Alexandria's fighting men joined the 17th Virginia Infantry Regiment. This monument, located in the middle of the city's main street, marks the spot where the first volunteers formed to march off to meet the Federal threat at a place called Manassas.

Washington and Prince streets.

17th Virginia Infantry Monument, Alexandria.

CHRIST CHURCH

One of the most famous Episcopal churches in Virginia, this building dates back to the colonial days. Robert E. Lee was confirmed here, and it is asserted that on April 21, 1861, following morning services, Lee met with representatives of Gov. John Letcher, who tendered him command of all of Virginia's military forces. In the graveyard behind the church are the remains of the South's ranking general, Samuel Cooper, and Confederate diplomat James Murray Mason. A mass grave of Confederate dead is also located here.

Two blocks north of the 17th Virginia monument, at Washington and Cameron streets.

STABLER-LEADBETTER APOTHECARY STORE

A metal plaque on the outside wall explains that here, in October 1859, Lt. Jeb Stuart handed a message from the secretary of war to U.S. Army Col. Robert E. Lee directing Lee to proceed at once to quell a disturbance by John Brown at Harpers Ferry.

105 S. Fairfax Street, four blocks east of Washington Street.

Custis-Lee Mansion, Arlington National Cemetery.

BOYHOOD HOME OF ROBERT E. LEE

Here the future Confederate general spent much of his boyhood. The home, built in 1795, is lavishly furnished with early nineteenth-century pieces. Once open to the public, this site is now a private residence and no longer available for touring.

From Washington Street, go a half-block on Oronoco to No. 607.

ARLINGTON   NE 2

Since 1965, Arlington County has erected 52 historical markers to indicate the sites of Civil War forts, hospitals, and other notable buildings. Fragmentary remains of a few of the forts still survive on private properties, yet the growth of the Washington suburban area has taken a deadly toll of the scenes of yesteryear.

ARLINGTON NATIONAL CEMETERY

This is understandably the most famous of the federally administered cemeteries. Eighty-one Union generals lie buried here, as well as Robert Todd Lincoln and Confederate Gen. Joseph Wheeler. One monument stands over the mass grave of 2,111 Federal dead. Sprinkled throughout Arlington are special Medal of Honor gravestones. (This highest of American awards originated during the Civil War.) At Jackson Circle, near the rear of the cemetery, are 250 Confederate soldier-graves. In their midst is an impressive bronze monument created by noted sculptor Sir Moses Ezekiel, who lies buried nearby. Individual auto tours of the cemetery are not permitted. Tourmobiles traverse the area on a regular schedule; rider fee.

The cemetery's visitor center is at the base of the hill at the south end of Arlington Memorial Bridge.

CUSTIS-LEE MANSION

George Washington's step-grandson built this home on an estate that is now Arlington National Cemetery. In 1831 Robert E. Lee married Mary Randolph Custis inside the Greek Revival mansion, and the couple made their home there for thirty years before the war. Visits to the home are part of any tour of the national cemetery.

The mansion sits atop a hill overlooking the Potomac River, the cemetery, and Washington, D.C.

FORT MYER

Established in 1863 as an earthwork named Fort Whipple, this fort was designated to be maintained as a permanent post after the war. Renamed to Fort Myer in 1880, it is the only remaining defense of the Northern capital still in use. Stationed here is the 1st Battle Group, 3d Infantry Regiment, which provides guard details for funerals of presidents and other dignitaries.

The main entrances are on U.S. 50, immediately behind the national cemetery.

FAIRFAX COUNTY   NE 3

This is a large and increasingly metropolitan area which nevertheless contains a number of varied Civil War sites. Unfortunately, they are scattered throughout the county. The attractions below are listed in a sequence whereby the visitor will travel roughly in an arc west from Arlington and ending near the southern outskirts of Alexandria. However, to make this swing will require patience to negotiate driving through always-heavy traffic.

FORT MARCY

Another anchor in the wartime defenses of Washington, this site is now operated by the National Park Service. It is presently in a natural state, with interlinking earthworks visible for several hundred yards. Interpretive markers, cannon, and a picnic area are at this overlook on the Potomac River.

Located on the north side of the George Washington Memorial Parkway, just east of the McLean exits.

FREEDOM HILL FORT

Off the beaten path here is an excellent example of a Civil War redoubt. This fortified picket enclosure was designed for 100 men and was used to guard Federal camps from raids by such Confederates as Mosby's Rangers. The interpretive markers are unique and outstanding.

Take Virginia 123 south toward Vienna. Two-tenths of a mile south of the intersection with Virginia 7, turn right (north) on Old Court House Road for 0.3 miles; the fort is on the left.

FAIRFAX COURTHOUSE

This was a famous building seen often in Mathew Brady photographs of the war period. It was used as a signal post and headquarters building throughout the Civil War.

Located in downtown Fairfax at the intersection of Virginia 123 and 236.

MARR MONUMENT

This stone marker pays tribute to Capt. John Q. Marr, killed early in the war on that spot. The two boat howitzers flanking the monument were captured by Confederates at the battle of First Manassas.

Located on the courthouse grounds.

MOSBY'S CAPTURE OF STOUGHTON

In a daring midnight raid on March 8–9, 1863, Capt. John S. Mosby and 30 Virginia troopers galloped into Fairfax. Federal Gen. Edwin Stoughton was taken prisoner as he lay ignominiously asleep in bed. The small band of Southerners also seized 32 other Federals, 58 horses, plus arms and equipment. This performance first called attention to Mosby's potential as a partisan ranger. The raid is marked by a monument; behind this is the Dr. William Gunnell House, where Stoughton was spending the night. The private residence is identified by a marker at the street.

Located 2 blocks west of Fairfax Courthouse on Virginia 236 (Little River Turnpike).

CONFEDERATE CEMETERY MONUMENT

Large markers denote the graves of known and unknown Confederate dead. During the Civil War, the cemetery was the site of a Union stockade.

From the Fairfax courthouse, proceed 4 blocks west on Virginia 236, then turn into the cemetery.

SAINT MARY'S CHURCH

This simple Catholic church, in a picturesque setting, was where Clara Barton (founder of the American Red Cross) tended scores of wounded Federal soldiers during the 1862 Second Manassas campaign. The field between the church and the railroad became an outdoor ward for innumerable injured soldiers.

Continue south on Virginia 123 from the Fairfax courthouse for approximately 3 miles. Turn right on Fairfax Station Road, 0.2 miles before crossing the Southern Railway overpass. The church is visible from Virginia 123.

POHICK CHURCH

Completed in 1774, Pohick Church was for decades a familiar landmark in the northern Virginia area. George Fairfax, George Washington, and George Mason served as vestrymen. During the Civil War, the church was in a sort of no-man's land, and

Pohick Church, Fairfax County, photograph by Francis Benjamin Johnston.

it suffered extensive damage—including much carving of initials on the soft sandstone walls. The graffiti is quite visible today.

When Virginia 123 terminates at I-95, proceed north on the interstate to Lorton Road. Exit there and go east to the dead end, then left (north) on U.S. 1 for 1 mile. The church is on the right.

U.S. ARMY ENGINEER MUSEUM

Like all armed services museums, this one has exhibits pertaining to the full scope of American military history. Some displays treat of engineering matters in the 1860s.

Located inside Fort Belvoir at 16th Street and Belvoir Road. Entrances to the fort are along U.S. 1 north of Pohick Church.

FORT WILLARD

This property, recently acquired by the Fairfax County Park System, offers a superb example of an earthen fortification in an unimproved state. Fort Willard was another of the 68 forts that encircle Washington. It provides a beautiful view of the Potomac River. Although situated now in a residential area, the site will undergo restoration in the near future.

Traveling north from Pohick Church, continue 9.5 miles up U.S. 1 to Beacon Hill Road. (A shopping center is on the west side of the intersection.) Go east on Beacon Hill Road for 1.1 miles to a stoplight, then left on Fort Hunt Road for 0.5 miles. Turn left again, this time on Glen Drive. Proceed 0.2 miles, bearing left at the fork near the top of the hill. The road will circle around the site of the fort.

OX HILL OR CHANTILLY

This area was the scene of a bitter rear-guard action at the close of the Second Manassas campaign. Fighting in a driving rain and severe thunderstorm, Confederates under Stonewall Jackson defeated their opponents and cost the lives of the Union commanders, Isaac Stevens and Philip Kearny.

Much of the current battlefield is lost to development, but a small memorial park, maintained by Fairfax County, contains monuments to the two fallen Federal generals. A state marker and other signage provide interpretive information.

Ox Hill Battlefield Park is located at 4134 West Ox Road, adjacent to Fairfax Towne Center.

DUMFRIES   NE 4

Confederate cavalry general Jeb Stuart targeted this area in his last major raid. Although unsuccessful in capturing the Union supply base, he moved through the region securing prisoners and war material before returning to the Fredericksburg area.

A state marker is located on U.S. 1, 1.62 miles north of Joplin Road.

MANASSAS   NE 5

Railroads from the south and west merged at Manassas and made the junction a point of major importance to both sides. Who controlled the railhead in essence controlled northern Virginia. On a hot Sunday in July 1861, the first major land battle of the Civil War took place here. The fighting forces were more akin to armed mobs than to armies. That the battle lasted the better part of a day and was marked by courage and determination on both sides was a tribute to Americans as a whole. In the Confederate victory, Gen. Thomas J. Jackson gained his nickname, "Stonewall."

Thirteen months later, on much of the same ground, occurred the battle of Second Manassas (or Second Bull Run, as Northerners called it). Jackson was instrumental in holding Gen. John Pope's army at bay until Lee arrived to drive the Federals from the field. Three days of combat produced almost 24,000 casualties. This smashing Confederate success cleared the way for Lee's first invasion of the North.

MANASSAS NATIONAL BATTLEFIELD PARK

The National Park Service has done a commendable job in maintaining portions of the two battlegrounds. A visitor center, displays, and guides are available to the public. The equestrian statue of Jackson atop Henry House Hill is a moving sight.

From I-66, turn north on Virginia 234. The NPS visitor center entrance is between I-66 and U.S. 29.

MANASSAS MUSEUM

Open only in the afternoons, this display presents a history of

Stone bridge spanning Bull Run, Manassas National Battlefield Park.

the rail-junction town. While the emphasis is on the war years, there is an expanded physical presence and interpretive emphasis. Admission charge.

9101 Prince William Street in Manassas.

STRATFORD HALL   NE 6

This birthplace of Robert E. Lee stands on a cliff high above the Potomac River. The home has been restored and holds many furnishings of the Lee family. Admission charge.

Proceed 40 miles from downtown Fredericksburg east on Virginia 3 to the junction with Virginia 214. Turn left and continue 1.1 miles to the estate.

FREDERICKSBURG   NE 7

Situated at the falls of and at a critical bend of the Rappahannock River, Fredericksburg had been a chief port for the Shenandoah Valley since colonial times. Two major battles were fought within its limits, and the town changed hands no less than seven times during the war.

BATTLEFIELDS

The first large-scale struggle for control of the city occurred on a cold Saturday in December 1862 when Federals made more than a dozen assaults against Lee's strong entrenchments. Fighting raged until nightfall. The result bordered on a massacre and prompted Lee to state during the battle: "It is well that war is so terrible—we should grow too fond of it." Losses in the Army of the Potomac exceeded 12,000 men; Confederate casualties were less than half that number.

In May 1863, as part of the Chancellorsville campaign (see C8), Union troops again attacked Marye's Heights at Fredericksburg. This time they were successful in driving the Southerners from their works.

The starting point for touring these sites is the National Park Service visitor center. It is located on the battlefields at the base of Marye's Heights, on which some 15,000 Federal soldiers are now buried. Available at the NPS center are a new slide-movie, exhibits, and guided tours. A 7-mile drive on an NPS road provides an almost-constant view of Confederate trenches as well as

Rebel caisson destroyed by Federal shells at Fredericksburg, May 3, 1863, photograph by Andrew J. Russell.

a better understanding of the extraordinary length of the 1862 battle line.

From I-95, take Virginia 3 east for 1.3 miles. Turn right near the bottom of the hill onto Sunken Road and proceed for 2 blocks. The visitor center and parking lot are on the left.

CONFEDERATE CEMETERY

Established in 1865 by the Fredericksburg Ladies Memorial Association, this burial plot contains the graves of 2,000 Southern soldiers (only 330 of whom have been identified). In this relatively small cemetery lie the remains of six Confederate generals: Seth M. Barton, Dabney H. Maury, Abner M. Perrin, Daniel Ruggles, Henry H. Sibley, and C. L. Stevenson.

Continue eastward on Virginia 3 toward downtown Fredericksburg. The cemetery is adjacent to the highway at the intersection of William and Washington streets.

CHATHAM

This eighteenth-century Georgia mansion is now the headquarters of the Fredericksburg and Spotsylvania National Military Park. Known during the war as the Lacy House, the imposing structure was a front-line headquarters for a number of Federal generals, including Edwin V. Sumner and Joseph Hooker. A variety of exhibits is open to the public. The front lawn offers a panoramic view of Fredericksburg.

Follow Virginia 3 eastward through Fredericksburg. Immediately after crossing the Rappahannock River, turn left at the first stoplight. Proceed 0.1 miles and turn left onto Chatham Lane, which leads to the parking lot for the mansion.

WHITE OAK CIVIL WAR MUSEUM

Converted into a museum from a one-room schoolhouse, the White Oak Museum features artifacts and exhibits focusing on items associated with soldiers from both sides who passed through the region. Admission charge.

Across the street from the museum is the White Oak Primitive Baptist Church, organized in 1789, and used as a hospital during the war.

The museum is located approximately 5 miles east of I-95. Follow the Warrenton Road to Falmouth and proceed on Route 218 to the site at 985 White Oak Road.

CHANCELLORSVILLE-WILDERNESS NE 8

Within a 15-mile radius of Fredericksburg is the greatest concentration of preserved battlefields in Virginia. This area was the scene of intense fighting for more than two years, with at least 600,000 men engaged in combat during that period.

SALEM CHURCH

This unobtrusive sanctuary, originally constructed in 1844, was the focal point of bitter fighting on May 3–4, 1863, as Union reinforcements from Fredericksburg sought to come to the aid of Gen. Joseph Hooker and the Army of the Potomac at Chancellorsville. Although the church has undergone extensive restoration, its walls still show the marks of battle. Paintings, exhibits, and artifacts enhance the church grounds. The site is administered by the National Park Service.

1.4 miles west on Virginia 3 from the I-95 intersection.

ZOAN BAPTIST CHURCH

A modern building occupies the site of the wartime wooden structure that was sometimes erroneously noted as Zoar or Zion on period maps. The church stands on a swell of ground which was Hooker's farthest advance toward attacking Lee's flank. From there the Federals retreated back to Chancellorsville, thereby leaving themselves susceptible to counterassault.

From Salem Church, continue 2 miles west on Virginia 3. The church is on the left (south) side of the highway.

CHANCELLORSVILLE

Considered Lee's greatest victory, Chancellorsville is located in a 72-square-mile area of dense woods and thick underbrush known as the Wilderness. Here Federal General Hooker's at-

Scene on the U.S. Ford Road (Battle of Chancellorsville) on the Night of April 30, 1863, drawing by Edwin Forbes.

tempt to turn Lee's left flank inexplicably lost its momentum. Lee, though woefully outnumbered, dispatched Stonewall Jackson on a counterflank march that caught the Union army by surprise. The battle began with skirmishes on May 1, 1863, and lasted the better part of three days. Over 30,000 men were killed, wounded, or captured. The irreplaceable Jackson was among the fatalities.

The National Park Service visitor center at Chancellorsville provides an excellent introduction and tour-start for the battle-field. The best way to see these grounds is by personal automobile tour, and CDs are available for purchase. Even the precise route of Jackson's 12-mile flank march can be followed.

The visitor center is 4 miles west on Virginia 3 from Zoan Baptist Church (or 7.4 miles from the junction of Virginia 3 and I-95).

WILDERNESS BATTLEFIELD

In 1864 the Army of the Potomac, with the General-in-Chief Ulysses S. Grant personally directing its operations, started southward again. Using a strategy similar to Hooker's the previous year, the Federals tried anew to turn Lee's left (western) flank. On May 4 the Union army moved into the darkness of the Wilderness. Lee was waiting. The next two days saw 182,000 men viciously fighting in woods often set afire by bullets. This struggle produced 26,000 casualties and was little more than a momentary check to Grant's advance.

Regrettably, only pieces of the Wilderness battlefield survive today. NPS roads traverse a portion of the area and give access to a handful of roadside markers and monuments. An automobile is a must for visiting any part of the battleground.

Exhibits are at the Chancellorsville visitor center and on Virginia 20, 1.6 miles from its junction with Virginia 3.

SPOTSYLVANIA   NE 9

From the struggle in the Wilderness, both armies then staged a footrace for control of the vital road junction at Spotsylvania Courthouse. The Southerners barely arrived first and constructed hasty but heavy earthworks. In the next fourteen days (May 8–21, 1864), a number of Federal attacks were made in an effort to break the Confederate lines. The bloodiest engagement of the campaign came in the rain on May 12, when Federals temporarily overran a salient whose northwestern face was known thereafter as the "Bloody Angle."

Recent improvements by the National Park Service have made Spotsylvania among the most impressive of Civil War sites. Paved roads run along the works. A walking tour—complete with numbered stops—has been developed for the "Bloody Angle" area. Markers include a plaque showing where a 22-inch oak tree was felled solely by rifle bullets.

To reach Spotsylvania via Grant's advance, proceed west from Chancellorsville on Virginia 3 to the intersection with County 613. Turn left (south) on County 613 and continue 13.7 miles to the Y intersection and exhibit shelter.

If traveling to Spotsylvania from Fredericksburg, take Alternate U.S. 1 south to its junction with Virginia 208. Turn right and continue 6.6 miles to downtown Spotsylvania. At the T in-

tersection in the center of town, turn right on County 613 to reach the battlefield area.

SPOTSYLVANIA COUNTY MUSEUM

Housed in Old Berea Church, a small brick edifice that suffered heavy damage during the 1864 fighting, this museum contains relics from the battlefields, two dioramas, and other memorabilia. Close to the museum is a Confederate cemetery with the remains of scores of soldiers killed in combat nearby.

Located on Virginia 208 at the eastern edge of Spotsylvania.

CIVIL WAR LIFE—THE SOLDIER'S MUSEUM

The museum has multiple exhibits devoted to aspects of the Civil War that range from battlefield artifacts to music and photographs. The collection focuses on soldier life and includes a 20-minute presentation. Admission charge.

To reach the museum, take Exit 126 from I-95 onto U.S. 1 South and proceed to 4712 Southpoint Parkway, adjacent to the Spotsylvania County Visitor's Center.

MASSAPONAX CHURCH   NE 10

Built in 1859, the rectangular brick structure was a rendezvous point in a number of troop movements, especially in Grant's 1864 Wilderness–to–Cold Harbor campaign. The building is best remembered because of a series of photographs taken of Grant and the ranking generals in the Army of the Potomac, all seated informally in the yard on church pews.

From the intersection of U.S. 1 and Virginia 208 south of Fredericksburg, drive south 3.6 miles on U.S. 1. The church is located on the west side of the highway.

GUINEA STATION   NE 11

It was at this railhead—on the afternoon of May 10, 1863—that Gen. Thomas J. ("Stonewall") Jackson died of pneumonia after being accidentally shot by his own men during the second day's

Massaponax Church "Council of War," with Gen. Grant examining map held by Gen. Meade, May 21, 1864, photograph by Timothy H. O'Sullivan.

combat at Chancellorsville. Jackson had been brought here following the battle. He was placed in the white clapboard office building of Fairfield, the Chandler plantation. This extremely pious commander died approximately on the Sabbath after uttering the words: "Let us cross over the river and rest under the shade of the trees." The house in which Jackson died, plus many furnishings (especially in the death room), are maintained by the National Park Service.

Leave I-95 or U.S. 1 at the Thornburg exit and proceed east on County 606 across the Richmond, Fredericksburg and Potomac Railroad. Bear left alongside the tracks to the parking lot for the house.

CARMEL CHURCH   NE 12

A modern edifice occupies the site where the wartime wooden church stood. The area of Carmel Church was the focal point of huge Army of Northern Virginia camps during the winter of 1862–63, and the church's name appears regularly through-out the war in dispatches relative to troop movements north of Richmond.

Located at the crossroads 15 miles south of Thornburg on U.S. 1.

GARRETT FARM   NE 13

On April 26, 1865, at this location, Presidential assassin John Wilkes Booth reached the end of his attempt to escape from Ford's Theater in Washington. Union soldiers surrounded Rich-ard Garrett's tobacco barn and shot the man who had killed Abraham Lincoln. Civil War Trails has designed a tour specifi-cally to follow Booth's escape route, with signage for the Garrett Farm to aid in interpretation.

State markers denote the area where the Garrett House once stood, approximately 2.5 miles south of the intersection of U.S. 301 and U.S. 17 near Port Royal and on the grounds of Fort A.P. Hill. The house site is in the median of U.S. 301 and the closest marker and access by footpath to the location is from the north-bound side of the road. Caution should be exercised due to traffic volume.

NORTH ANNA BATTLEFIELD   NE 14

During May 23–26, 1864, Grant launched a series of assaults in an effort to break Lee's entrenchments along the south bank of the North Anna River. The attacks failed, and the Army of the Potomac then veered southeastward and continued its advance on Richmond. Portions of the battlefield and earthworks are preserved and accessible to visitors and numerous interpretive markers can be found along the 2-mile walking trail in the 75-acre North Anna Battlefield Park.

The trail can be reached by traveling west along Verdon Road (Virginia Route 684) from U.S. 1 near Doswell Road (Virginia Route 685). U.S. 1 crosses the North Anna virtually in the center of the battle area, 5 miles south of Carmel Church.

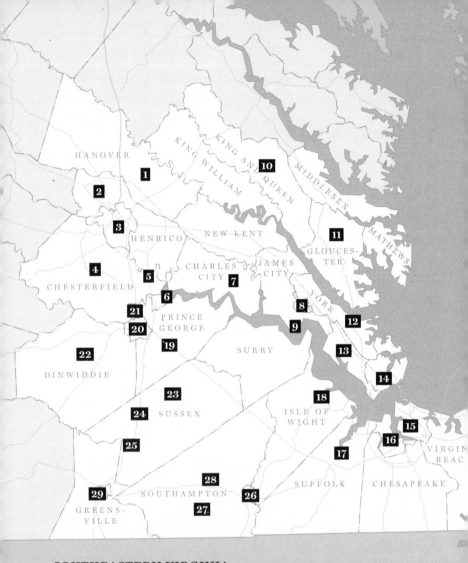

SOUTHEASTERN VIRGINIA

N
miles   10   25

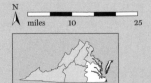

SOUTHEASTERN VIRGINIA

To crush secession and restore the Union meant that the Northern forces would have to take the role of invaders and conquer the South. Enormous Federal armies ultimately went into action, as did a naval blockade of the Southern coastline. In the Eastern theater—the area lying between the Appalachian Mountains and the Atlantic Ocean—this strategy caught Virginia in a mighty vise. In addition, Northern leaders earnestly believed that if the Confederate capital could be seized, the Southern nation would collapse. Thus, for four years Richmond was the primary military objective of the North.

Two basic approaches to the capital existed: the overland route by way of Manassas and Fredericksburg and the water route via Hampton-Yorktown and westward up the 80-mile peninsula formed by the York and James rivers. Federal armies tried both approaches, in one instance utilizing the largest amphibious operation that the modern world had ever seen. Losses unprecedented in American history accumulated through the years before Virginia eventually succumbed.

HANOVER COUNTY   SE 1

At this site James Ewell Brown ("Jeb") Stuart received his commission as major general and organized the cavalry corps of Lee's army. On the courthouse lawn is a monument bearing the names of 1,138 county men who fought for the Confederacy. Some 50 names were inadvertently omitted, including Maj. Thomas Doswell and Surgeon Robert Coleman.

Located in Hanover, 12 miles north of Richmond, at the intersection of U.S. 301 and Virginia 54.

SUMMER HILL

Here, in June 1862, ladies prepared for burial the body of Capt. William Latané, the first Confederate fatality on Stuart's "Ride around McClellan." Latané fell on the road between Hanover and Old Church. The solemn occasion is immortalized in the painting *The Burial of Latané* by William D. Washington (1864), which was widely reproduced after the war as a powerful symbol of the "Lost Cause" ideology. As of 2010, the formerly unmarked grave in the family cemetery bears a headstone to the fallen warrior.

At various times during the war, Federal Gens. McClellan, Sheridan, and Grant occupied the home, and it was also used for a time as a military hospital. The modest frame house still belongs to the Newton family, but visitors are welcome.

One mile south of Hanover on U.S. 301, turn left (east) on County 605 and go 7 miles. A sign points to Summer Hill.

MALBOURNE

Buried here is the Southern firebrand and famed agronomist Edmund Ruffin. Noted for his contributions prior to the war in agricultural science, he was zealous in his advocacy of the Southern cause. In June 1865, as he contemplated the outcome of the war, he found that he could not bear the defeat of the Confederacy and took his own life.

U.S. 360, 8.9 miles northeast of Mechanicsville.

HENRICO COUNTY   SE 2

YELLOW TAVERN

On May 11, 1864, near a way station along the Brock Turnpike, occurred a sharp cavalry fight between the horsemen of Gens. Philip Sheridan and Jeb Stuart. The thirty-one-year-old Confederate commander was shot near the end of the action and died the following day from loss of blood. The spot where the "Gray Cavalier" was mortally wounded is marked and maintained by the United Daughters of the Confederacy.

From I-95 North, drive west 0.4 miles on Parham Road to the intersection with U.S. 1. Turn north for 2.1 miles. Turn right (east) on Francis Road and go 0.5 miles to Telegraph Road, then bear right on Telegraph Road for 0.1 miles. The Stuart Memorial is on the right-hand side of the road.

DAHLGREN'S RAID

In the spring of 1864, Union cavalry raiders under Col. Ulric Dahlgren approached the Confederate capital. Their scheme, which called for releasing captured Federals from Confederate prisons and generally creating havoc in Richmond in conjunction with other troops under Gen. Judson Kilpatrick, failed in part because of inadequate cooperation and unexpected resistance from local forces.

A state marker is located at Horsepen Road, between Three Chopt Road and Patterson Avenue in the West End of Richmond. A fight at Green's Farm occurred near Three Chopt, and Dahlgren moved down Westham Plank Road (now Cary Street Road) toward the city until he reached Hick's Farm, about 5 miles out from the Capitol.

FORT HARRISON

Attacked on September 29, 1864, as part of Benjamin Butler's Bermuda Hundred campaign, the fort fell to the Federals and became incorporated in the Union defense lines. Prominent in the successful assault on neighboring New Market Heights, east of the fort, were United States Colored Troops (USCT).

The fort is part of the Richmond Battlefields system and is located on U.S. 5, 4.5 miles southeast of the city.

RICHMOND   SE 3

Richmond was literally the heart of the Confederacy. The capital of both the Southern nation and the Confederacy's most important state, Richmond also became the chief manufacturing center in the wartime South, the major rail junction in the Upper South, and hence the sole target for four years of the North's principal army. Major military campaigns in 1862 and 1864–65, a number of Federal raids, and a population that quadrupled the 1860 total of 38,000 inhabitants kept Richmond in turmoil and instability for most of the war. Yet the city stood proud and defiant through all adversity until its abandonment in April 1865.

Today Richmond has more historic attractions than any other city in the South. The visitor who wishes to see all Civil

War points of interest should allow a minimum of two days for touring.

RICHMOND NATIONAL BATTLEFIELD

The Richmond National Battlefield Park Visitor's Center is located in the complex that once held Tredegar Iron Works, in what served as the Pattern Building erected in 1867. Exhibits and an audiovisual program at the National Park Service building provide a summary of the years of heavy fighting waged for control of Richmond.

A free, easy-to-understand brochure is available for a self-guided 100-mile drive through the major battlefields around the capital. This drive is essential for serious students of the Civil War. The tour includes Seven Pines, where Confederates checked McClellan's 1862 advance on Richmond in a two-day battle fought largely in mud and swamps. With the wounding at Seven Pines of Gen. Joseph E. Johnston, Robert E. Lee assumed army command and promptly counterattacked. A succession of battles known as the Seven Days followed as Lee sought desperately but in vain to destroy the Federal army and end the war in Virginia.

Lincoln statue above the Richmond National Battlefield Park Visitor's Center.

Today only traces remain of Mechanicsville, Gaines's Mill, Savage's Station, White Oak Swamp, Frayser's Farm, and Malvern Hill. Yet in these engagements the Confederates reversed impending defeat and, at a staggering cost of 25 percent losses, repulsed the second major Union effort to seize Richmond.

Also on this tour is the partially restored battlefield of Cold Harbor. Here, on June 3, 1864, Gen. U. S. Grant rashly ordered dawn frontal assaults against Lee's heavily fortified lines. What ensued has been termed the worst slaughter of Americans in the nation's history. Some 7,200 Federals were shot down in 20 minutes. Thereafter, Grant resumed his flanking movements, crossed the James, and invested Petersburg. A number of forts involved in the 1864–65 besiegement are part of the auto tour.

The Richmond National Battlefield Park Visitor's Center is located at 470 Tredegar Street.

AMERICAN CIVIL WAR CENTER

Opened in 2006, the American Civil War Center is housed in the revitalized Gun Foundry building and offers exhibits that interpret Union, Confederate, and African American perspectives of the conflict. The central theme of the exhibits, "In the Cause of Liberty," allows visitors to follow the causes and chronology of the Civil War as well as its outcome and legacies.

500 Tredegar Street.

LINCOLN STATUE

A statue of a seated President Abraham Lincoln and his son Tad is located nearby, in front of a wall with the engraved inscription "To Bind Up The Nation's Wounds." The image captures Lincoln's arrival from City Point on April 4, 1865, accompanied by Tad, whose twelfth birthday the occasion also marked.

On the ground overlooking the Richmond National Battlefield Park Visitor's Center and the American Civil War Center.

HISTORIC TREDEGAR IRON WORKS

Chartered in 1833 and opened in 1837, the iron works struggled in its earliest years until a former soldier and future Confederate general Joseph R. Anderson assumed a relationship with the company in 1841 that flourished into ownership. Critical as a Southern industrial facility, Tredegar produced armored plates for the ironclad CSS *Virginia* and ordnance for the Confederacy.

The remains of some of the facilities of the vital manufacturing plant are preserved, including those utilized by the American Civil War Center and the Richmond National Battlefield Park's Visitor's Center.

CHIMBORAZO MEDICAL MUSEUM

The former site of the Richmond Battlefields National Park Service Visitor's Center, and still the location for its headquarters, this museum occupies the area of wartime Chimborazo Hospital, where 76,000 patients treated during the course of the Civil War made it the largest military hospital ever constructed. Exhibits familiarize visitors with medical practices and include a diorama of the layout of the enormous operation.

3215 E. Broad Street (the city's main thoroughfare).

MUSEUM OF THE CONFEDERACY

This two-building complex consists of a new exhibit hall and the three-story home that served as the Confederate White

House. The largest extant collection of Confederate artifacts is here, including the field uniforms of Gens. Lee, Jackson, Stuart, and Joseph E. Johnston. The 1818 Brockenbrough mansion, which served as the official residence of President Jefferson Davis, has been extensively renovated to appear as it did during the war years. Admission charge.

The White House and its adjacent museum are located at the corner of East Clay and 12th streets, 2 blocks north of Broad Street.

Office of Jefferson Davis, White House of the Confederacy, Richmond.

VALENTINE MUSEUM

Built in 1812 and donated to the City of Richmond 70 years later, this is a depository principally of costumes and other fine arts material. The chief Civil War attraction is a plaster cast of Edward V. Valentine's most famous sculpture, the recumbent figure of Gen. Robert E. Lee (commissioned for the chapel at Washington and Lee in Lexington). Admission charge.

The home and its adjoining historic structures stand at the southwest corner of Clay and 11th streets, a block west of the Museum of the Confederacy.

STATE CAPITOL

Designed by Thomas Jefferson, this building was the seat of the Confederate government. It was inside the marble edifice, in April 1861, that Robert E. Lee assumed command of all Virginia forces. In February 1862 Jefferson Davis delivered his inaugural address at the base of the Washington statue in the northwest corner of the Capitol grounds; this statue became the major symbol on the Confederate Seal. Also on the grounds of the Capitol are bronze likenesses of Confederate notables Gen. Stonewall Jackson, Gov. William Smith, and Surgeon Hunter McGuire. A statue of Robert E. Lee can be found in the Old House of Delegates chamber (where he accepted the command of Virginia troops in 1861), together with busts of other prominent Virginians. Guided tours of the Capitol itself are conducted on a regular basis.

Capitol Square is situated one block south of Broad Street between 9th and 12th streets.

SAINT PAUL'S EPISCOPAL CHURCH

This stately sanctuary, dedicated in 1845, is widely known as the "Church of the Confederacy." Jefferson Davis was confirmed here early in the war, and on April 2, 1865, he was attending morning prayer services when he received word from Lee that the Richmond-Petersburg defenses had been broken. The Lee Memorial Window and pew plaques are some of the church's leading Civil War features.

Across the street from Capitol Square, on the southwest corner of Grace and 9th streets.

STEWART-LEE HOUSE

The Stewarts made their home available to Confederate Gen. Robert E. Lee for his use during and immediately following the war. Lee's invalid wife, Mary, was in the home when the Confederates evacuated Richmond, and refused to leave even when fire reached the house next door. General Lee returned to the home, where famed photographer Mathew Brady managed to convince him to pose.

707 E. Franklin Street.

MONUMENT AVENUE

This wide boulevard is so named because of five large statues interspersed along its route. The monuments are of Jeb Stuart, Robert E. Lee, Jefferson Davis, Thomas J. Jackson, and Matthew Fontaine Maury.

The avenue is basically a continuation of Franklin Street, with its eastern end at Lombardy Street. It is parallel to, and 2 blocks south of, Broad Street.

BATTLE ABBEY

Now the headquarters of the Virginia Historical Society, this majestic building was built as a Confederate memorial hall in 1913. On display are Southern portraiture and weapons. One room houses a gigantic mural series entitled "Four Seasons of the Confederacy" by French artist Charles Hoffbauer, depicting battle scenes in Virginia and utilizing the seasons of the year to represent the four years of conflict. Within the building is probably the best research library on the Civil War in the Old Dominion.

This museum–reference library is at 428 N. Boulevard, 4 blocks south of Broad Street.

HOLLYWOOD CEMETERY

Second in renown only to Arlington National Cemetery, this 115-acre tract opened in 1849 and derived its name from large holly trees located on the grounds. Here are found the largest number of distinguished Virginians buried in one place. Hollywood also contains the graves of 15,000 Confederate soldiers who perished

Statue of Robert E. Lee by Jean Antonin Mercie on Monument Avenue, Richmond.

during the war. A map-guide to the more prominent graves (including those of three presidents—James Monroe, John Tyler, and Jefferson Davis) is available at the cemetery office just inside the gate. The driveways are quite narrow, and funeral services may occasionally impede travel in some sections.

The cemetery entrance is at Cherry and Albemarle streets. From Broad street, proceed south on Belvidere (U.S. 1-60-301) for 7 blocks. Then turn right (west) on Albemarle Street for 3 blocks.

BELLE ISLE

On this island in the James River stood one of the war's chief prison camps. Some 6,000 Federals were confined here at the prison's peak. The island is now open to the public from the north side (near Tredegar) via a footbridge that runs under U.S. 1/301. An emergency access bridge also reaches the island from the south from James River Park, which has operational authority over the site.

As one continues southward on Belvidere and crosses the river, Belle Isle is visible just below the bridge on the right-hand (west) side.

OAKWOOD CEMETERY

Although less famous than Hollywood Cemetery, Oakwood is the final resting place for numerous Southern officers and men, including Charles Hasker, the only man to survive when the Confederate submarine *Hunley* sank to the bottom of Charleston Harbor during one of its test runs before its historic rendezvous with the USS *Housatonic* off Charleston, South Carolina, in 1864.

3101 Nine Mile Road; from I-64 East take Exit 193A to Nine Mile Road (Virginia 33W).

CHESTERFIELD COUNTY   SE 4

BERMUDA HUNDRED CAMPAIGN

In 1864, as Lee tried to prevent Grant from reaching Richmond, Union Gen. Benjamin Butler landed 39,000 Union troops at Bermuda Hundred plantation on the James River hoping to sever the Richmond and Petersburg Railroad and threaten the Confederate capital from that direction. The Bermuda Hundred campaign fizzled and the Confederates contented themselves

Artillery on Drewry's Bluff, Richmond.

with having successfully "bottled" Butler's Army of the James between the James and Appomattox rivers by constructing a series of earthwork defenses known as the Howlett Line. Various state markers and Civil War Trails signs offer interpretation of this campaign.

A Howlett Line marker is located on U.S. 10, east of I-95, heading toward Hopewell.

HALFWAY HOUSE

Built in 1760, the Halfway House was so named because it was the mid-point between Richmond and Petersburg. Fighting during the Bermuda Hundred campaign occurred near this structure, which also served as Butler's headquarters at this time.

The house is located on the east side of Jefferson Davis Highway (U.S. 1) and several markers denote its importance.

DREWRY'S BLUFF (FORT DARLING)   SE 5

Although included in the automobile tour of the Richmond-area battlefields, the beauty and the comparative isolation of this site make it deserving of special mention. The bluff is on a bend in the James River, 7 miles south of Richmond. Early in 1862, Confederates erected strong fortifications here to guard the water approach to the capital. On May 15 of that year, Southern cannoneers at Drewry's Bluff (or Fort Darling, as it is sometimes called) repulsed an attack by a Federal fleet that included the celebrated ironclad *Monitor.* The Confederate naval academy was established here the following year, and Drewry's Bluff was the scene of more fighting in May 1864.

A walking tour of the elaborate remains of the fort has been developed by the National Park Service. A painting and huge Columbiad cannon are on display at the installation's most scenic spot.

Located south of downtown Richmond off Jefferson Davis Highway (U.S. 1). Bear left on County 656—Bellwood Road. Immediately beyond an overpass, turn left on Fort Darling Road and follow the signs to the parking area.

CITY POINT   SE 6

Through the latter part of the war, this port facility was among the most active in the country in support of the Union operations against General Lee's defense of Petersburg and Richmond. The grounds of Appomattox Manor, overlooking the James and Appomattox rivers, served as Ulysses Grant's headquarters for the duration of the siege of Petersburg. A small reconstructed cabin offers a glimpse at the general's accommodations, which were spartan despite visits from his family and President Abraham Lincoln.

Appomattox Manor—a unit of the Petersburg National Battlefield Park—contains a visitor contact station for the site with a brief audiovisual program for orientation.

North side of Route 10, in Hopewell.

CHARLES CITY COUNTY   SE 7

No major action took place in this county, but Federal armies passed through the district—and left their marks upon it—in both 1862 and 1864.

WILSON'S WHARF

Perhaps the most dramatic event in the county was the May 24, 1864, raid of Confederate cavalry under Fitzhugh Lee against a Union depot at this site. United States Colored Troops repulsed the assault and completed work on a fortification designated Fort Pocahontas. The fort site is in the private hands of descendants of President John Tyler, but access is possible for group tours and special events.

A marker is located on John Tyler Memorial Highway (Virginia Route 5) east of Sturgeon Point Road (County Route 614). The fort itself is located in close proximity to Sherwood Forest Plantation, President John Tyler's home.

SALEM CHURCH

One of the oldest Methodist churches in America, Salem served as a field hospital for wounded and sick soldiers on both sides

Grant's Headquarters at City Point, from *Harper's Weekly,* 1865.

in 1864. The building no longer stands, but a cemetery adjacent to the site contains the remains of a number of Confederates—including a member of the "C.S. Detective Corps."

Starting at the courthouse in Charles City, drive west on Virginia 5 for 5.6 miles. Turn north on County 609 for 3.5 miles. The cemetery and site of Salem Church are on the left.

BERKELEY PLANTATION

This was the birthplace of President William Henry Harrison. Gen. George B. McClellan used the home for a headquarters during the 1862 Peninsula campaign. When Federal Gen. Daniel Butterfield occupied the mansion that same year, he composed the bugle call now known as "Taps." The plantation served as a hospital and signal station. On most wartime maps, Berkeley is called Harrison's Landing. Admission charge.

The entrance to the plantation is 6.6 miles west of Charles City on Virginia 5.

SHIRLEY PLANTATION

An estate whose beginnings date from the early 1600s, Shirley Plantation has a history that spans 300 years. Anne Hill Carter, the mother of Robert E. Lee, was born here, and the future Confederate general enjoyed many visits to Shirley. The home was a Federal hospital during McClellan's 1862 advance on Richmond. When Federal troops ransacked the home later that summer, Lee reputedly became angrier than at any other time in

Shirley Plantation, Charles City.

the Civil War. The mansion is still owned by the Carter family. Admission charge.

From Charles City, the plantation entrance is 9.9 miles west on Virginia 5.

WILLIAMSBURG   SE 8

This first capital of Virginia became a key point in the Confederate defenses of the peninsula. Here, on May 5, 1862, the initial battle of the Peninsula campaign took place. The major fighting raged east of the town, although skirmishes occurred in the streets and on the campus of the College of William and Mary. The Wren Building, the main building on the campus, was burned by Federals; in 1895 the federal government made partial restitution.

ARCHER'S HOPE

At this inlet of the James River, Confederates threw up gun emplacements to challenge any Federal ships advancing up the river. Vestiges of these works are evident today.

From Williamsburg, proceed 5.1 miles south on the Colonial Parkway.

JAMESTOWN   SE 9

Here, where America began, will be found two extensive remains of Southern earthworks. Legend has it that the trenches were constructed in 1861 by slaves from Surry County plantations across the river. Admission charge.

The Civil War reminders are prominently situated along the waterfront on Jamestown Island, close to the reconstruction of the original fort.

KING AND QUEEN COUNTY   SE 10

Having been thwarted in his raid against Richmond, Union Col. Ulrich Dahlgren paused here to camp on March 2, 1864, but Confederates ambushed his force and killed him. On his person were documents that were supposed to have linked him to a plot to free Union prisoners of war, burn the city, and kill prominent leaders, including President Jefferson Davis.

A state marker is located on Virginia 631, 2.5 miles northwest of King and Queen Court House.

GLOUCESTER COUNTY   SE 11

This county was the scene of several minor skirmishes during the war. A monument on the courthouse lawn at Gloucester contains the names of all local men who lost their lives in the conflict on the Confederate side.

GARDNER MONUMENT

Dedicated in 2005, a stone marker honors Medal of Honor recipient Private James Daniel Gardner of the 36th United States Colored Troops for his role in the Battle of Chaffin's (Chapin's) Farm, September 29, 1864.

Located in the Court Circle at U.S. 17 Business and Blair Road.

GLOUCESTER TOURIST INFORMATION CENTER

Among the information available here is a list of all graves of known Confederate soldiers in the county, as well as directions to the various cemeteries in the area.

Located in the old Debtors Prison on the west side of U.S. 17 Business in downtown Gloucester.

WARE CHURCH

Women of the community kept this Episcopal church open and functioning regularly throughout the war. It remained free from harm in spite of Federal occupation and occasional skirmishes.

From the center of Gloucester, proceed 0.2 miles on Virginia 14. The church is on the south side of the highway.

ABINGDON CHURCH

Not as fortunate as Ware Church, this house of worship suffered the indignity of being used as a stable. However, the federal government later reimbursed the congregation for damages done.

Located on U.S. 17, 1.5 miles south of Gloucester and just beyond the junction with County 614.

GLOUCESTER POINT

Extensive earthworks were here for the duration of the Civil War. Some remnants are visible opposite Tindall's Point Bridge.

Continue south from Gloucester on U.S. 17 to the bridge spanning the York River. Gloucester Point stands at the north end of the bridge.

YORKTOWN   SE 12

Early in the war, Confederates began fortifying the Virginia Peninsula against a possible Federal advance on Richmond. Three defense lines were built from the James to the York rivers. Though time has erased all traces of the first and third positions, much of the second, strongest line of works, extending from Fort Crafford on Mulberry Island to Yorktown, remains in evidence. The Confederate defenses included man-made lakes as well as entrenchments.

It was at Yorktown in March–April 1862, that Federal Gen. George B. McClellan landed his massive Army of the Potomac for an advance on Richmond up the peninsula. This amphibious operation involved the transfer from Washington to Yorktown of 121,500 men, 59 batteries of artillery, 15,000 animals, and 1,100 supply wagons, plus tons of military goods too numerous to itemize.

Memorial Day ceremony at Yorktown National Cemetery.

COLONIAL NATIONAL HISTORICAL PARK

Here Gen. John B. Magruder, commanding Southern forces on the peninsula in 1861, reinforced many of the Revolutionary War trenches utilized by the British. It is now difficult to ascertain precisely which earthworks in the Yorktown park figured in both wars, but this National Park Service site offers a stunning view of earthen defenses.

From U.S. 17, just east of the town of Yorktown, proceed on the Colonial Parkway 0.7 miles to the park headquarters. Trenches known to have been employed in the Civil War will be on the right as you enter the parking lot.

YORKTOWN NATIONAL CEMETERY

Established in 1866, this cemetery contains 2,200 graves, mostly of Union dead. A small Confederate graveyard is located nearby.

Located on County 704 inside the Yorktown battlefield park.

JONES MILL POND EARTHWORKS

Here will be found another example of the elaborate trench network erected by the Confederates in their defense of the peninsula.

From the Yorktown Visitor Center at the park, go 9.2 miles on the Colonial Parkway.

NEWPORT NEWS   SE 13

Today's teeming metropolis is a far cry from the village that existed at the time of the Civil War. Yet in spite of its size at the time, Newport News figured prominently in the 1861–62 Virginia campaigns.

NEWPORT NEWS PARK

The largest municipal park east of the Mississippi River, this recreation area also contains superb reminders of the Civil War. Confederate General Magruder made extensive use of existing dams in preparing his defense lines. He also erected other levees to enable the Confederates to flood the lowlands in case of a Federal advance. Inside the park is Dam No. 1, the scene of a sharp fight on April 16, 1862, when Vermont troops attempted unsuccessfully to break the Confederate position. This unusual battlefield remains basically as it was. An interpretive center and walking tours are accessible to the public.

More avid and athletic history buffs can take a 3-mile hike in the park to Wynn's Mill, where stand in virginal state the most impressive earthworks in Virginia.

Exit from I-64 onto Virginia 105 East. Drive 0.1 miles to the intersection with Virginia 143. Turn left (west) and continue for 0.3 miles to the park entrance. The interpretive center is 0.9 miles inside the park on the right, with the battlefield extending on both sides of the road.

ENDVIEW

This Georgian-style house dates from 1769 and served as a Confederate hospital during the 1862 Peninsula campaign. Admission charge.

Use Exit 247 to reach Yorktown/Lee Hall Road in Newport News. The house is located at 362 Yorktown Road.

LEE HALL MANSION

Completed in 1859, this structure served as headquarters for Confederate Gens. John B. Magruder and Joseph E. Johnston during the Peninsula campaign. Admission charge.

Located at 163 Yorktown Road.

FORT EUSTIS

There are two Civil War attractions inside this army base. The first is the U.S. Army Transportation Museum, which though slanted heavily toward recent military history, includes several Civil War exhibits. The second is Fort Crafford, a star-shaped bastion on Mulberry Island which anchored the right flank of the Confederacy's main defense line across the peninsula. The earthworks and gun emplacements of Fort Crafford are remarkably well preserved. However, the site is an isolated area of Fort Eustis. Persons wishing to visit the riverside area should check first with Transportation Museum officials to determine when Fort Crafford is open for inspection.

To reach the fort, take Virginia 105 west from I-64 for 1.4 miles. Follow museum signs inside the installation.

THE MARINERS' MUSEUM

Artillery pieces and exhibits on Civil War naval affairs form a small part of this extraordinary museum. A new interpretive center devoted to the Union ironclad *Monitor* includes a life-sized replica of the vessel and numerous artifacts raised from its watery grave off the outer banks of North Carolina, including its iconic turret. Allow extended time to make a thorough visit. Admission charge.

Take Exit 258A from I-64 and travel 2.5 miles to the intersection of Warwick Boulevard and J. Clyde Morris Boulevard (Avenue of the Arts). Continue straight through the intersection and turn left onto Museum Avenue.

WAR MEMORIAL MUSEUM OF VIRGINIA

This large depository has 20,000 indoor and outdoor exhibits documenting Virginia soldiers from pre-Revolutionary times to the present. Uniforms, accoutrements, and artwork of the 1860s are displayed. Admission charge.

Leave I-64 at the junction with U.S. 258 and proceed south for 3.4 miles. Turn west on U.S. 60 for 0.4 miles. The museum is on the south side of the highway.

MONITOR-MERRIMACK OVERLOOK

This magnificent view of Hampton Roads is the point from which scores of persons gathered on March 9, 1862 to watch the duel between the USS *Monitor* and the CSS *Virginia* (formerly the USS *Merrimack*). Weather permitting, Forts Monroe and Wool, the Norfolk Naval Yard, and other points are clearly visible from this overlook.

At Exit 265A on I-64, proceed south toward Newport News on Virginia 167 for 4.6 miles to the second roadside historical marker. The first marker, "First Battle of Ironclads," is in the wrong place and should be located two miles farther west.

CAMP BUTLER

This is the site of an early Federal installation that was used in the last months of the war as an internment camp for Southern prisoners of war. A monument commemorates the Confederate captives who perished while incarcerated there.

CONGRESS-CUMBERLAND OVERLOOK

This site offers a view of the area in which the Union wooden warships *Congress* and *Cumberland* were lost in an engagement with the Confederate ironclad *Virginia* on March 8, 1862, prior to the celebrated "Battle of the Ironclads" that occurred the next day.

Located in Christopher Newport Park, 26th Street and West Avenue, in Newport News.

HAMPTON   SE 14

On June 10, 1861, just outside Hampton, occurred the battle of Big Bethel. It was the first significant engagement of the war in Virginia. Two months later, Confederates raided Hampton to prevent its occupation by Federals; in the ensuing action, the town was virtually demolished.

SYMS-EATON MUSEUM

This small depository contains uniforms and interpretive exhibits on Hampton during the war period. The Hampton Information Center is directly across the highway.

From I-64, go east toward Fort Monroe on U.S. 258 (Mercury Boulevard) for 1.5 miles.

BIG BETHEL

Here some 4,000 untested Federals attacked 1,500 equally green Confederates. Two hours of confused fighting followed before the Northerners fled the field. Unfortunately, the site of the battle is now beneath the Big Bethel Reservoir, inside Langley Air Force Base. Two monuments and small cemetery are the only reminders of its wartime significance.

Take U.S. 258 south from I-64 to the first stoplight. Turn right (west) on Todds Lane for 1.6 miles to the intersection of Big Bethel Road, then continue 3.3 miles to the markers.

FORT MONROE

Any visit to the lower peninsula should include a lengthy stop at this base, traditionally known as "The Gibraltar of Chesa-

Illustration of the Battle of Hampton Roads between the USS *Monitor* and the CSS *Virginia*, from Joseph Joel, *Rifle Shots and Bugle Notes*, 1884.

peake Bay." Construction of the casemated and moat-encircled fort began in 1819 and took fifteen years to complete. Robert E. Lee was a principal engineer. During the Civil War, the fort was headquarters for Federal Gens. Benjamin F. Butler and George B. McClellan. Lincoln and Grant both were guests there, and Confederate President Jefferson Davis was imprisoned in one of the casemates following his May 1865 capture.

Of interest today are the Jefferson Davis Casemate Museum (the logical and necessary starting point), Robert E. Lee's quarters, the Chapel of the Centurion, the Lincoln Gun, and the view of the harbor entrance. Following the fort's decommission as a military base, new interpretive material will include the story of runaway slaves, known at the time as "contraband of war," a phrase popularized by Union Gen. Benjamin Butler.

From I-64, take either Virginia 143 or 169 and follow signs to Fort Monroe. Military police at the fort's gate will provide directions to the Casemate Museum inside the old bastion.

FORT WOOL

Situated on a man-made island in the middle of the Hampton Roads channel, this abandoned army base is often called "Rip Raps" after the shoal on which it rests. The original installation was known as Fort Calhoun and was completed in 1858 after

Ruins of the Norfolk Navy Yard, 1864, photograph by James Gardner.

twenty-eight years of labor. Designed to strengthen the defenses of the harbor's entrance, Fort Wool was a focal point in the 1862 Federal bombardment of Norfolk. President Lincoln watched the artillery barrage from its ramparts.

The island is now owned by the City of Hampton and clearly visible from any vantage point. The site is accessible by harbor tour boat and private watercraft.

NORFOLK   SE 15

Ten percent of Norfolk's 14,000 residents perished in an 1855 epidemic of yellow fever. The town—Virginia's principal port—had barely recovered from this tragedy when civil war exploded in its midst. In April 1861 Federals burned and abandoned the navy yard. Union forces reoccupied Norfolk in May 1862 and exercised strong and sometimes brutal control over the city for the remainder of the war.

HAMPTON ROADS NAVAL MUSEUM

The museum is dedicated to a wide swath of American naval history, but a portion of the exhibit gallery is specifically devoted to the Civil War, and particularly the story of Hampton Roads in the conflict. Artifacts include pieces associated with the CSS *Virginia* and 1862 antagonist USS *Cumberland,* as well as the Confederate commerce raider *Florida.*

The museum is located on the second floor of Nauticus: The National Maritime Center, on Waterside Drive. There is no admission charge, but visitors should indicate that they plan to visit only the museum to avoid the Nauticus entry fee. There is no on-site parking, but an ample number of spots can be found in the city within walking distance.

Visitors will find it easiest to follow signage to Nauticus, although the route differs slightly based on direction of approach.

CONFEDERATE MONUMENT

This 1907 memorial pays tribute to the men of Norfolk who served in Confederate forces.

Intersection of Main Street and Commerce Place.

OLD TOWN HALL

Here, in an elaborate ceremony, Federal troops triumphantly raised "Old Glory" when the city was captured in 1862. The building is now the MacArthur Memorial.

Located on MacArthur Square in the downtown area.

ELMWOOD CEMETERY

This cemetery contains a "West Point" section that includes a statue that is purported to be inspired by Norfolk-born William Carney, a member of the United States Colored Troops and Medal of Honor recipient from his service as a flag-bearer in the assault on Battery Wagner outside Charleston, South Carolina.

Located off East Princess Anne Road.

PORTSMOUTH   SE 16

The Portsmouth Naval Shipyard has been an active producer of warships for over a century. Amid its bustling activity today are several reminders of achievements of yesteryear.

PORTSMOUTH NAVAL SHIPYARD MUSEUM

Numerous relics and displays here include items pertaining to the South's first ironclad warship, the CSS *Virginia*.

Located at 2 High Street, alongside the Elizabeth River.

U.S. NAVAL HOSPITAL

A stone cairn memorializes some 300 men lost in the destruction of the USS *Cumberland* and *Congress* in a March 8, 1862, attack by the CSS *Virginia*. On adjacent grounds to the hospital are the graves of many Confederate and Federal soldiers.

North end of Green Street.

SUFFOLK   SE 17

At least eight skirmishes were fought in and around Suffolk. Yet the town's most conspicuous period came during April 11–May 4,

1863, when Confederates under Gen. James Longstreet, assuming that Gen. John Peck's 25,000 Federals inside the town were about to embark on a northern drive toward Richmond, lay siege to Suffolk. This movement never materialized, and the siege proved ineffective, although the Confederates used the opportunity to scour the region, including counties in northeastern North Carolina, for badly needed supplies and foodstuffs.

RIDDICK'S FOLLY

General Peck's headquarters during the Suffolk campaign was in this home. The dwelling dates back to 1839. Admission charge.

The home and adjacent Nathaniel Riddick Law Office are located at 510 N. Main Street.

OLD NANSEMOND COUNTY COURT HOUSE

The Union army used this structure as a barracks and headquarters for much of the war. It now houses local law courts.

Easily recognizable, the courthouse stands at 524 N. Main Street

GODWIN HOUSE

Constructed in 1830 but recently altered by minor improvements, this dwelling was used as a hospital by Federal forces during the siege of the city. It is not open to the public but may be seen from the roadway.

504 W. Washington Street.

CEDAR HILL CEMETERY

In use many years before the outbreak of civil war, this burial ground contains scores of graves from the conflict of the 1860s. The cemetery serves as the final resting place for Brig. Gen. Laurence S. Baker, a North Carolina cavalry commander who settled in the area as a railroad executive. A Confederate monument is one of the dominant markers in the cemetery. A Civil War Trails sign located at the monument interprets the 1863 "Siege of Suffolk."

Intersection of Main Street and Constance Road.

RIVER POINT

The remains of a portion of the earthwork fortifications that General Peck and his men erected are preserved overlooking the Nansemond River and facing the ground over which significant military action took place during the Siege of Suffolk in April–May 1863.

This area can be reached by turning off Constance Road at the River Point complex, and via the wooden overlook accessed by a stone footpath between the buildings.

HILL'S POINT OR BATTERY HUGER

Known at the time of the sectional conflict as the "Old Fort" because of its affiliation with the defense of the Nansemond River prior to the Civil War, Hill's Point became the scene of the most prominent combined arms engagement along the river during the siege of Suffolk. Utilizing converted ferryboats as gunboats and transports, Union troops under Brig. Gen. George W. Getty succeeded in surprising and capturing a Confederate battery on April 19, 1863, seriously damaging Longstreet's prospects for taking the town itself.

The fort is located and preserved as part of a complex associated with the Nansemond River Golf Club. The area can be reached by turning off Route 10 onto Hillpoint Boulevard, but the fort can be reached only by permission.

PROVIDENCE METHODIST CHURCH

A little country church on a crossing point for two of the many wartime roads that ran through Nansemond County, Providence Church served as field hospital and stable to forces from both sides.

Located on U.S. 460 west of Suffolk.

SMITHFIELD   SE 18

FORT HUGER

Constructed in 1861 on a bluff along the James River, this fortification was part of the river defenses for Richmond and named for the regional commander, Confederate Gen. Benjamin Huger. Southern forces abandoned the position in May 1862 under pressure from the movements associated with George McClellan's Peninsula campaign.

Fort Huger Historical Park is located on the northern end of the Isle of Wight County and is operated by the county. The site is open from 8:00 AM until dusk daily and has easy parking access, although a short walk is required to reach the earthworks themselves. The fort also provides an excellent platform for viewing the modern "graveyard" of ships on the James River.

Eight miles north of Smithfield, Fort Huger can be reached from Route 10 by traveling northward on Fort Huger Drive for 0.75 miles, turning right on Tyler's Beach Road (0.8 miles), left on Woodmere Road (0.3 miles) and another left on Lawnes Neck Drive (1.4 miles). The parking area and entrance are on the right on Talcott Terrace.

FORT BOYKIN

Dating back to 1623, this is one of the oldest fortifications in America. The earthen work was improved during the War of 1812 to its present seven-pointed-star design. In 1862 fire from Federal gunboats forced the Southern garrison to abandon the installation. Confederate soldier-poet Sidney Lanier wrote at least two poems while stationed here in the war's first months. The 15-acre tract is operated by Isle of Wight County.

The fort is located 4 miles north of Smithfield. Take Business Route 10 from downtown to the junction with unpaved County 673. Proceed on County 673 to the intersection with County 705. The fort stands at that point alongside the James River.

ISLE OF WIGHT MUSEUM

The scene of several smaller scale military operations, Smithfield includes a museum that offers interpretation for these events as well as other elements of local history.

Located downtown at 103 Main Street.

Cattle Raid of Gen. Wade Hampton, drawing by Alfred R. Waud, 1864.

PRINCE GEORGE COUNTY   SE 19

"BEEFSTEAK RAID"

In September 1864 Confederate cavalry under Gen. Wade Hampton galloped behind Federal lines and captured an entire herd of cattle for Lee's starving army. The daring operation not only provided badly needed sustenance, but also a significant morale boost for the hungry Southerners. The motion picture *Alvarez Kelly,* featuring William Holden and Richard Widmark, immortalized the raid for generations of moviegoers.

A marker dedicated to the event sits at the intersection of Virginia 609 and 635.

PETERSBURG   SE 20

Next to Richmond, Petersburg was the scene of more Civil War action than any other community in Virginia. The nine-month siege of the city in 1864–65 remains the longest such operation on American soil. Some 35 miles of parallel earthworks extended in unbroken lines from east of Richmond to southwest of Petersburg. Constant pounding by Federals of Lee's thin but defiant ranks during the siege produced over 65,000 Northern and Southern casualties. Throughout the long campaign, Confederate Gen. John B. Gordon noted, "Lee's Miserables" were occupied in "fighting famine from within and Grant from without." The dozens of engagements fought around Petersburg make the area the largest battlefield in America.

HISTORIC PETERSBURG INFORMATION CENTER

This starting point for any tour of the city, the center offers personal assistance as well as printed material on the Petersburg area.

Washington Street, just to the west of I-95 at Exit 52.

PETERSBURG NATIONAL BATTLEFIELD

A variety of attractions makes this one of the National Park Service's most popular sites. The visitor center has a 17-minute lighted map presentation of the Petersburg campaign. Behind the center are a display of cannon tubes, an original artillery fort, and a seacoast "Dictator" type mortar. An automobile tour with numbered stops winds past forts and rebuilt works and culminates at the Crater, scene of one of the war's most unique and costly battles. For those who wish to examine a larger and more undeveloped segment of the siege lines, a self-guided, 16-mile auto tour passes along sites on both public and private property. Detailed leaflets on all of these points of interest are obtainable at the park headquarters.

From I-95 proceed east on Virginia 36 for 2.4 miles to the battlefield park entrance.

U.S. ARMY QUARTERMASTER'S MUSEUM

This large and elaborate display contains weapons, emblems, and equipment spanning all of America's wars.

The museum is inside Fort Lee, which is adjacent to the battlefield park. Signs along Virginia 36 East provide easy directions.

BLANDFORD CEMETERY

The massed graves of 30,000 Confederates are in this huge cemetery, which was established over 270 years ago. Local tradition insists that Memorial Day was first marked here on June 9, 1866. No visit to Petersburg is complete without a tour of Blandford Church. The two-century-old building, located just inside the main gate of the cemetery, is a memorial to Confederate dead. Fifteen Tiffany stained-glass windows radiate a beauty —especially in late afternoon—that can scarcely be described, and must be seen. A nearby museum offers a slide program and exhibits pertaining to the church's history.

From Exit 52 off I-95, follow U.S. 301 south for 0.2 miles. The cemetery is on the left.

SIEGE MUSEUM

One of the state's more formal displays, this museum highlights the events and hardships of the long Federal siege of the city. Movie star and Petersburg native Joseph Cotten narrates a film which dramatically retells the city's wartime story.

Located at 15 W. Bank Street, the museum is in a renovated area of the downtown. Take Exit 52 west from I-95.

SAINT PAUL'S EPISCOPAL CHURCH

A marker denotes the pew where General Lee worshipped during the nine-month campaign for Petersburg. The marriages of two other Confederate generals, William H. F. ("Rooney") Lee (the commanding general's son) and George E. Pickett, took place in this church. A stained-glass window dedicated to the memory of Robert E. Lee, a nave that remains as it looked at the time of the war, and "the only notable antebellum set of church bells in Virginia" are other features of Saint Paul's.

Leave I-95 at Exit 52. Proceed west for 5 blocks, then turn right to 110 N. Union Street.

TURNBULL HOUSE

This reconstructed home served as Lee's headquarters from November 1864 until the Federal breakthrough in April 1865. It is privately owned.

Located on the north side of U.S. 1, approximately 1 mile south of the Appomattox River.

13-inch "Dictator" mortar in front of Petersburg, 1864.

COLONIAL HEIGHTS   SE 21

VIOLET BANK

This Federal-style house was built in 1815. It served as head-quarters for Robert E. Lee from June to November 1864.

303 Virginia Avenue, east of U.S. 1 in Colonial Heights.

DINWIDDIE COUNTY   SE 22

More than 45 engagements took place within this county in the last ten months of the war. Dinwiddie County is estimated to have over 50 miles of extant fortifications as well as remnants of 50 forts and batteries. Directions to the more accessible of these sites may be obtained at the Petersburg National Battlefield headquarters.

POPLAR GROVE NATIONAL CEMETERY

Situated on ground where severe fighting occurred in 1864 for control of the nearby railroad, this cemetery contains the graves of more than 6,000 soldiers—4,000 of them unknown.

Located on County 675, a half-mile south of the Petersburg city limits and just east of I-85.

PAMPLIN HISTORICAL PARK

This impressive park and interpretive center sits on the location of a Union penetration of the Southern lines near Petersburg.

The Confederate defense of the town collapsed from this point on April 2, 1865, also prompting the evacuation of Richmond. A hallmark of the visit is the National Museum of the Civil War Soldier, as well as trails leading past a section of the Southern trenches. Living history programs and reconstructed earthworks bolster the historical experience. Admission charge.

The entrance to the complex is located off U.S. 1, south of Petersburg.

FIVE FORKS

At this obscure point, on the afternoon of April 1, 1865, Gen. Philip H. Sheridan launched massive Federal assaults that broke the Southern lines after a nine-month stalemate. Lee's outnumbered army, starving on its feet, then started on a 100-mile "corridor of sorrows" that would end at Appomattox. The battleground constitutes a unit of the Petersburg National Battlefield Park and has a Visitor Contact Station just beyond the critical intersection on Courthouse Road on the right, with maps, exhibits, and a short interpretive film. Ample parking is available and there is no admission to this visitor's center.

A roadside marker about Five Forks is on U.S. 460, 5 miles west of Sutherland. The battlefield can be reached by proceeding west from Sutherland on U.S. 460 for 6 miles, then south on County 627 for 4 miles to its junction with County 613.

BURNT QUARTER

Sheridan's headquarters during the battle was in this plantation home of the Gilliam family. The house was also the scene of at least one session of Gen. G. K. Warren's subsequent court of inquiry. Burnt Quarter is well maintained and contains many of the furnishings of the Civil War period.

Situated on County 613, 1 mile west of the Five Forks junction.

DONNAN HOUSE   SE 23

The cattle pilfered in Hampton's "Beefsteak Raid" were driven southwestward past the Donnan House, which is now in private hands. Confederate troopers asked directions here; in return for the information, they gave the destitute family a cow that was too disabled to be driven farther.

County 626, just east of the junction with Virginia 35.

STONY CREEK   SE 24

This small community was the scene of several engagements in the last year of the war. In one such action (June 28, 1864), Federals retreated so hastily that they discarded furniture, silverware, livestock, personal effects, and 1,000 contrabands—all of which they had confiscated elsewhere. This pillaging later led to a subsequent Federal investigation.

A historic marker is located at the intersection of U.S. 301 and Virginia 40.

SAPPONY CHURCH

West of Stony Creek, and south of the intersection of Virginia 40 and County 681, is Sappony Church, the site of a June 1864 skirmish. Today a circular patch in the pediment marks where a shell struck the building. A Bible grazed by a rifle ball can also be seen here.

A Civil War Trails marker connects the site to the 1864 Wilson-Kautz Raid and is located at Virginia 40 and Concord Sappony Road adjacent to the church.

JARRATT   SE 25

Little more than a village in 1861–65, this railroad stop was burned in May 1864 by Federal cavalry. Seven months later, the tracks in and around here were wrecked beyond repair. The only dwelling in Jarratt that was not destroyed, the Humphrey Grigg Tavern, was spared the torch reputedly because the Federals used it as a headquarters.

The tavern, now privately owned, is at Old Halifax Road and County 631 in Jarratt.

FRANKLIN   SE 26

A significant link on the river and rail network between Norfolk and Weldon, North Carolina, the town served as a depot and commercial center along the Blackwater River. Following the fall of Norfolk and Suffolk, Union cavalry patrols raided the area frequently to assess Confederate strength on the "Blackwater Line," and a joint operation with Union gunboats reached the outskirts of the town on October 3, 1863, only to be thwarted by obstacles placed in the river and by armed citizens.

From Suffolk take Highway 58 heading West. Exit at Pretlow Street, Highway 714, going toward the Franklin Historic District. Turn right on South Street, Highway 258. Interpretative markers are located at the riverfront.

NEWSOMS   SE 27

This little Virginia community marks the home of Union Gen. George Henry Thomas, who chose to remain with the Union when his native state seceded. Popularly known during the

conflict as the "Rock of Chickamauga," Thomas raised the ire of family and friends for his decision, but became one of the most successful Federal field commanders. The home, known as Thomaston, is in private hands, but contains markers noting the connection to the general and a brief biographical sketch of his life.

From Route 58, take the exit for Virginia 671, General Thomas Highway, to Cypress Bridge Road. Turn right and take a left shortly on Thomaston Road. The house will be 0.5 miles on the right.

Gen. George Henry Thomas.

COURTLAND   SE 28

In antebellum days, Courtland was called Jerusalem. Near here on the night of August 21, 1831, a slave revolt led by Nat Turner and a band of his followers claimed the lives of 57 whites, mostly women and children. Hastily organized posses brutally suppressed the uprising, and Turner and a dozen of his followers were tried, convicted, and hanged. The Nat Turner insurrection was the bloodiest overture to civil war in Virginia.

The properties bordering Virginia 35 for approximately three miles north of Courtland were the scene of the insurrection.

BAPTIST CHURCH

This structure was one of the town's most prominent buildings during the war. It was pressed into service as a hospital in 1863 when an epidemic of measles swept through the nearby army camps. Several soldiers (mostly members of Hood's Texas Brigade) succumbed to the disease and are buried in the cemetery behind the church.

Located in the center of Courtland at 22264 Main Street.

EMPORIA   SE 29

During the Civil War, modern-day Emporia was known as Hicksford. The town served as a trading post starting in the early 1700s and flourished with the establishment of a rail line connecting Petersburg and Weldon, North Carolina.

HICKSFORD RAID

Commanding a sizable force, Union Gen. G. K. Warren attempted to disrupt the Petersburg Railroad by wrecking portions of it, including a bridge over the Meherrin River at Hicksford. Wade Hampton and Fitzhugh Lee could do little to stop the raid, but when Warren withdrew work parties hastily repaired the damage.

A state marker is located on Main Street (U.S. 301) at Meherrin River Park.

NELSON

AMHERST

BUCKINGHAM

8

6

CUMBERLAND

2

POWHATAN

9

7

4

3

10

APPOMATTOX

AMELIA

BEDFORD

CAMPBELL

PRINCE
EDWARD

NOTTOWAY

CHARLOTTE

LUNENBURG

PITTSYLVANIA

5

BRUNSWICK

1

HALIFAX

MECKLENBURG

11

SOUTH CENTRAL VIRGINIA

1 Lawrenceville
2 Derwent
3 Amelia
4 Sailor's (Sayler's) Creek Battlefield Historical State Park
5 Staunton River Bridge

6 Buckingham County
7 Appomattox
8 Amherst
9 Lynchburg
10 Bedford
11 Danville

N

miles 10   2

SOUTH CENTRAL VIRGINIA

This section of the Piedmont was the center of the Upper South's money crop—tobacco—which to Johnny Rebs and Billy Yanks alike was either a luxury or a good for barter, worth its weight in gold. Southside Virginia did not feel the hard hand of an invading army until the last week of hostilities. Still, the conflict altered appreciably and permanently the lives of the small farmers and merchants who comprised the bulk of the region's society. These Virginians had been among the most ardent secessionists, and it is ironic that the Civil War ended in their midst.

LAWRENCEVILLE   SC 1

The county courthouse, a red brick structure with tall Ionic portico, was the scene of a personal drama toward the war's end. Union troops were approaching the town and its fall was imminent. The county clerk, realizing the impossibility of hiding the huge volumes that contained the county's records, spread his Masonic apron on his desk and left his office door open. Federals briefly occupied the town, then departed. The clerk returned to his office to find that the records had not been touched.

Located on U.S. 58 Business in downtown Lawrenceville.

DERWENT   SC 2

In July 1865, Lee and his family moved to this modest two-story frame house to escape the crowded atmosphere of postwar Richmond. He lived here for three months before departing for Lexington to assume the presidency of Washington College.

On U.S. 60 proceed 8 miles west of Powhatan, turn right (north) on County 629 to Trenholm, then follow the signs.

AMELIA   SC 3

On April 4, 1865, Lee's retreating and impoverished army reached this town in hopes of securing food from cars of the Richmond and Danville Railroad. No supplies materialized, forcing the Southern army to resume its westward march the following day. The Jackson Library in Amelia contains some items of interest, and in the clerk's office at the county courthouse is an unofficial roster of all Amelia County soldiers.

CONFEDERATE MONUMENT

One of the more impressive memorials to Virginia Confederate soldiers, this monument stands on the courthouse lawn. Adjacent to it is a monument to Lamkin's Battery which contains a mortar that saw action at the Crater in Petersburg.

Near the intersection of Washington and Court streets.

SAILOR'S (SAYLER'S) CREEK BATTLEFIELD
HISTORICAL STATE PARK   SC 4

Here took place the final major battle of the war in Virginia. On April 6, 1865, Federals encircled the rear third of Lee's retreating force. Fighting lasted through the afternoon and resulted in more than 7,000 Southerners captured, including eight gener-

The Last of Ewells Corps, April 6, drawing by Alfred R. Waud, 1865.

als and a large number of high-ranking officers. As broken fragments of Confederate columns stumbled to catch up with what was left of the main body, Lee looked at the scene and exclaimed, "My God! Has the army dissolved?" Today over 320 acres of the battlefield have been developed into a state park. A visitor's center is located on the battlefield near the site where the remnants of Gen. Richard Ewell's troops surrendered.

From U.S. 360, 9 miles west of Amelia, travel along Holly Farms Road (Route 307), then turn north on Sayler's Creek Road (County 617) for 1.7 miles to the park boundary. From U.S. 460 take County 617, crossing Holly Farms Road (Route 307).

HILLSMAN HOUSE

Scene of the staging ground for a Union assault against Ewell's Confederates entrenched above Little Sailor's Creek, the house served as a field hospital for the wounded of both sides from the April 6 engagement. With the family patriarch imprisoned after his capture at Spotsylvania, other family members and servants huddled in terror in the basement while the fighting raged around them.

On the Sailor's Creek battlefield, near Jetersville and Sayler's Creek Road (County 617).

LOCKETT HOUSE

This structure, still bearing the scars of nearby fighting late on April 6, 1865, served as a hospital as Union forces closed on retreating Confederate troops. Gen. John B. Gordon's command was providing rear-guard protection for the Southern wagon train when the Federals struck, costing the Confederates substantial numbers of prisoners and lost conveyances.

To reach the house from the Sailor's Creek battlefield, travel along Route 617 and turn left on James Town Road (Route 618). The dwelling is located just beyond the intersection with Route 619, on the left.

STAUNTON RIVER BRIDGE   SC 5

In June 1864 two Federal cavalry regiments attempted to sever the Richmond and Danville Railroad by destroying the high bridge over the Staunton River. An undersized Confederate regiment, assisted by 600 local citizens, repulsed the Federals after sharp fighting. A modern metal trestle now stands at the site, but remnants of earthworks can be found along the river's edge. On the lawn of the Legion Hall in downtown South Boston is a tube of one of the Confederate cannon used in the engagement.

To reach the Staunton River Battlefield State Park, travel from Kings Highway (U.S. 360) at Clover, then go north on Virginia 92. Turn onto Black Walnut Road (County 600) to go to the Clover Visitor's Center that serves as the main entrance for the park and provides closest access to Fort Hill, a Confederate earthwork on the south side of the river. A second visitor's center is located near Randolph and can be accessed directly by foot or bicycle along the railroad bed trail 0.8 miles in distance, or more circuitously by automobile (6 miles).

BUCKINGHAM COUNTY   SC 6

County 636, which traverses Buckingham County, is the main route that Lee's army followed on its way to a rendezvous with history at Appomattox. From Farmville, take Virginia 45 north for 5 miles, then left on County 636 at Raines Tavern. At a point 3.5 miles west on 636 is Clifton, the home where Gen. U. S. Grant spent the night of April 8, 1865, and where he corresponded with Lee about a possible surrender of the Confederate army. The home is not open to the public.

APPOMATTOX   SC 7

At this quiet village, far from the arenas of bloodshed, four years of war in Virginia came to a close. Lee's ragged army retreated to this point on April 8, 1865, only to find itself surrounded by the Federal Army of the Potomac. On the afternoon of the following day—Palm Sunday—Lee met personally with his Union counter-

McLean House, Appomattox Courthouse National Monument (*above*), print of Gens. Grant and Lee at Appomattox (*below*).

part in the McLean House. The terms of surrender offered by Grant and accepted by Lee were the most lenient for any civil war in history, with the result that the legacy of bitterness so associated with such conflicts did not mar this nation's history. The Civil War ended here, but it would be more appropriate to say that modern America began here. The National Park Service has restored a dozen buildings in this community. Several exhibits as well as convenient walking tours are available.

From U.S. 460 in present-day Appomattox, take Virginia 24 for 3 miles northeast to the park entrance.

AMHERST   SC 8

A county historical museum in Amherst has a display treating of the Civil War period. The museum is on Taylor Street, one block from Main Street and near the county courthouse.

Fourteen miles east of Amherst on U.S. 60 at the crossing of the James River stand the abutments of a covered bridge burned in 1865 by Sheridan's cavalry.

LYNCHBURG   SC 9

The junction of three rail lines and a major east–west canal made Lynchburg an important supply depot during the war. The town was also the site of two camps of instruction and several military hospitals, a rendezvous center for Confederate troops, and a brief military campaign in June 1864.

FORT EARLY

Named for Gen. Jubal A. Early, who commanded the Southern defenses and who made Lynchburg his home from 1869 until his death in 1894, this partially restored redoubt is the only earthen reminder of the battle of Lynchburg. A simple monument to Early stands nearby.

Remnants of Fort Early are located on Fort Avenue (U.S. 29 Business) and Vermont Avenue. The grounds are easily viewed but not open to the public.

SPRING HILL CEMETERY

Here will be found the graves of Confederate Gens. Early and James Dearing, cavalry commander Thomas T. Munford, Sen. John Warwick Daniel, and a child of Gen. Jeb Stuart.

Fort Avenue, between Lancaster Street and Wythe Road.

CONFEDERATE MONUMENT

Designed by James O. Scott of Lynchburg and erected in 1898, this statue of a Southern infantryman honors all sons of the area who served as soldiers in the war.

This marker is at the top of Monument Terrace and across the street from the Old City Court House (which is currently being developed into a museum of Lynchburg's history).

DANIEL MONUMENT

John Warwick Daniel served on Early's staff and received a serious wound at the battle of the Wilderness, but later enjoyed a distinguished career as orator and U.S. senator. This unique memorial to "The Lame Lion of Lynchburg" was the creation of Sir Moses Ezekiel, one of the most famous of the postwar sculptors.

Located at the intersection of Park Avenue, 9th Street, and Floyd Street.

JACKSON FUNERAL BOAT

A fragment of the hull of the canalboat *Marshall* is located in Riverside Park. This vessel transported the body of Gen. Stonewall Jackson from Lynchburg to his grave in Lexington.

Riverside park is located on a picturesque bluff overlooking the James River, at 2270 Rivermont Avenue.

SANDUSKY

Built in the Federal style in the early 1800s, this brick home served as the headquarters for Union Gen. David Hunter during the battle of Lynchburg, June 17–18, 1864. Members of his staff created a passageway to the roof which still remains, to view the fighting around Lynchburg.

757 Sandusky Drive.

BEDFORD   SC 10

A sparsely settled area at the time of the war, Bedford County nevertheless contributed over 600 artillerists and infantrymen to the Confederate cause. The town of Bedford (then known as Liberty) was heavily damaged by Federal troops during the June 1864 Lynchburg campaign.

CONFEDERATE MEMORIAL

This stone shaft, dedicated in 1909, honors all county men who served in the conflict.

Located on the west lawn of the Bedford County Courthouse, on Main Street in downtown Bedford.

BEDFORD CITY/COUNTY MUSEUM

In this relatively small depository are a number of artifacts from the Civil War period. Restricted visiting hours are in effect. Admission charge.

One block east of the courthouse, at 205 E. Main Street.

PIEDMONT HOSPITAL

Originally a boy's school that began operation in 1849, this building served as a military hospital for most of the war. It is now the Liberty Manor Home for the Elderly, but it retains its wartime appearance. Visitors may inspect the first floor of the premises.

812 E. Main Street.

LONGWOOD CEMETERY

Five Confederate hospitals were established in and around Bedford. Years after the war, the remains of soldiers who had died of sickness and wounds were placed in a single grave in this cemetery. Today a tall obelisk stands over the final resting place of 192 Southern soldiers and a Confederate nurse.

From Main Street in downtown Bedford, go north on Bridge Street for 0.3 miles. The cemetery is on the right.

DANVILLE   SC 11

This city was the western terminus during wartime for the vital Richmond and Danville Railroad. Situated at the falls of the Dan River, it too became an important supply base for Confederate military efforts in Virginia. In the last days of the war, six of Danville's tobacco warehouses served as prisons for captured Federal soldiers. The lack of necessities, plus a small-pox epidemic, led to the deaths of some 1,400 of the prisoners. When Lee's thin lines at Richmond and Petersburg broke under attacks on April 1–2, 1865, the Confederate government shifted to Danville, and for a week the city was the capital of the Southern nation.

Danville Museum of Fine Arts and History.

PRISONS

Two of the six warehouse-prisons still stand. Visitors will need local assistance in finding them.

300 Lynn Street and 514 High Street in the downtown area.

DANVILLE MUSEUM OF FINE ARTS AND HISTORY

This antebellum home of Maj. William T. Sutherlin, a Confederate quartermaster, is very often called "the last Capitol of the Confederacy." Jefferson Davis lived here during April 3–10, 1865, and it was from here that he issued his last presidential proclamation.

975 Main Street, west of the business district.

NATIONAL CEMETERY

Here will be found the graves of 1,100 Federals who died while prisoners of war.

721 Lee Street, alongside the tracks of the Southern Railway. From the Sutherlin Mansion, proceed south on Holbrook Avenue 6 blocks to the stop sign. Turn left onto Stokes Street and go one long block to the dead end. Turn right for one block, then left on Lee Street.

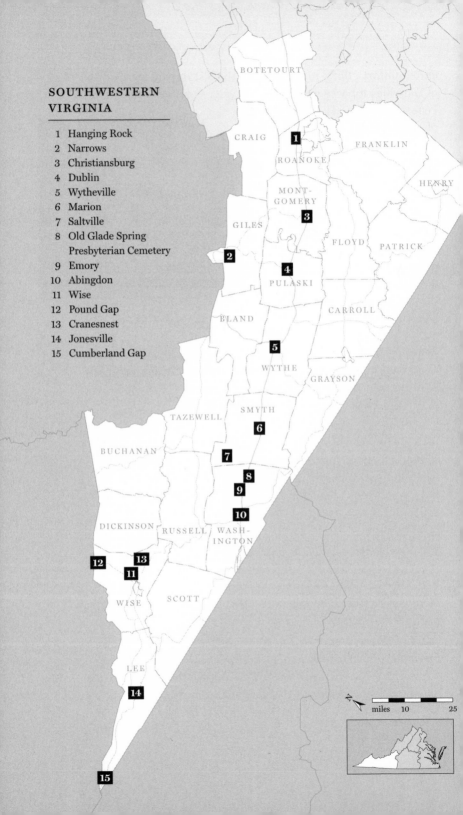

SOUTHWESTERN
VIRGINIA

1 Hanging Rock
2 Narrows
3 Christiansburg
4 Dublin
5 Wytheville
6 Marion
7 Saltville
8 Old Glade Spring
   Presbyterian Cemetery
9 Emory
10 Abingdon
11 Wise
12 Pound Gap
13 Cranesnest
14 Jonesville
15 Cumberland Gap

miles 10   25

SOUTHWESTERN VIRGINIA

Mountains isolate the southwestern tip of the Old Dominion from the rest of the state, and strongly divided sentiments characterized its people during the Civil War. Guerrilla activities on behalf of both sides were regular occurrences here. In addition, Federal horsemen slashed through the area in repeated efforts to neutralize the Virginia and Tennessee (now Norfolk and Western) Railroad, which linked Virginia with Tennessee and the entire western theater of operations. This area became the leading source for some of the Confederacy's most necessary resources: salt for its citizens, coal for its naval vessels, and saltpeter for gunpowder. While few visible signs of the war remain today, this southwestern area offers the most scenic drives in Virginia.

HANGING ROCK   SW 1

A plain, triangular-shaped monument stands at the site of a June 21, 1864, running fight between Gen. David Hunter's Federal army, retreating westward from Lynchburg, and Gen. Jubal Early's pursuing Confederates. At the time of the war, Roanoke (then called Big Lick) was an insignificant village straddling the Virginia and Tennessee Railroad.

Leave I-81 at Exit 141 and drive northward on Virginia 311 for 0.4 miles. The historical marker is on the right-hand side of the highway, with Hanging Rock itself directly across the road.

NARROWS   SW 2

This hamlet was one of the strategically important sites in southwestern Virginia. It is the most easily defended point along the vital New River (which, incidentally, is considered by many geologists to be second in age only to the Nile). Narrows remained in Federal hands until May 1864, when Confederates reoccupied the town and constructed a fort on the adjacent heights. Both sides used nearby, conspicuous East River Mountain as a signal station.

Present-day U.S. 460 passes through the narrows formed by the New River.

CHRISTIANSBURG   SW 3

This community was the scene of raids by Union Gens. W. W. Averell in 1864 and George Stoneman in 1865.

A state highway marker is located 0.5 miles east of I-81 on U.S. 11.

DUBLIN   SW 4

CLOYD'S MOUNTAIN

Union forces under Gen. George Crook clashed with Confederates under Gen. A. G. Jenkins here during a raid against the Virginia and Tennessee Railroad. Jenkins received a mortal wound in the fighting.

The site of the engagement is located 5 miles north of Dublin and to the west of State 100. Two state markers can be found on Virginia 100 near the battlefield.

WYTHEVILLE   SW 5

Wytheville's production of lead and its location on the railroad made it the scene of several military actions in 1863 and 1864. Union cavalry raiders under Gen. George Stoneman targeted the area, as well as the salt works at Saltville, for destruction in December 1864.

MARION   SW 6

This rail town was the scene of a sharp engagement between Stephen Burbridge and John C. Breckinridge over several days as part of Stoneman's 1864 raid in southwestern Virginia. An 1838 schoolhouse building is the setting for the Smyth County Historical Museum, where scores of artifacts—including a bullet-riddled Bible that saved the life of a Confederate soldier—may be seen.

The museum is located at 230 N. Church Street.

SALTVILLE   SW 7

Much of the common salt for the Confederacy came from this remote village, and its salt wells were extremely important to the embattled South. Confederates beat back a Federal attack here in October 1864, but two months later Union forces seized and destroyed the works. The wartime wells no longer exist, but brine ponds and the hills where the fighting occurred remain. A Salt Park located at the Washington–Smyth county line offers

Salt Park, Saltville.

interpretation of the salt-making process, as well as the fighting that occurred in that sector when George Stoneman approached in October.

Much of the area over which Union Brig. Gen. Stephen Burbridge, who led a force of 3,600 (including 600 U.S. Colored Cavalry) that clashed with 2,800 Confederates, remains, as well as a portion of the earthworks they defended, with Civil War Trails interpretation. A view from Elizabeth Cemetery, located on the left-hand side of the road, makes evident the natural obstacles that helped to secure the Southern left flank and provides a vista of the ground over which the Federals approached and the North Folk of the Holston River below. The aftermath of the battle sparked controversy, labeled the "Saltville Massacre" for the unnecessary deaths of troops there and at the hospital at Emory and Henry College. Ample parking exists for both the Salt Park and the Burbridge battlefield overlook. Care should be taken when driving through Elizabeth Cemetery.

To approach the area from the north, take Exit 35 on I-81 at Chilhowie, then proceed on Virginia 107 for 8 miles to Saltville. A magnificent view of the bowl-shaped area in which the town rests is available on this route.

From the south, use Exit 29 at Glade Spring, then proceed north on Virginia 91. This winding road will bring the visitor to the Salt Park and offers the best view of the high ground surrounding Saltville.

OLD GLADE SPRING
PRESBYTERIAN CEMETERY   SW 8

Situated behind a church established in 1772, this cemetery contains the remains of Gen. William E. ("Grumble") Jones, who was killed in the 1864 battle of Piedmont, and Dr. William L. Dunn, a surgeon with Mosby's Rangers.

Leave I-81 at Exit 29, proceed east a short distance to U.S. 11, then south for 0.2 miles.

EMORY SW 9

Many Confederate soldiers, either prostrate from illness or wounded in fighting at nearby Saltville, were brought here for treatment. The upper floors of Wiley Hall at Emory and Henry College served as a hospital for troops from both sides. The notorious Confederate guerrilla Champ Ferguson killed one of the incapacitated Union officers here in the aftermath of Burbridge's assault on Saltville.

Just west of the campus, on a hill overlooking the small community, 206 soldiers lie buried. A stone and bronze obelisk contains the names of all but two of the Confederates. These names correspond with numbered stones laid nearby.

Two of the best-known students associated with Emory and Henry, a small Methodist college founded in 1836, were future Confederate Gens. James Ewell Brown ("Jeb") Stuart and William E. ("Grumble") Jones.

From Exit 26 on I-81, drive west on County 737 and proceed 0.4 miles to the entrance of the college. To continue to the cemetery, pass the entrance and bear right at the railroad tracks toward the hamlet. Upon reaching the town, turn left on Linden Street (County 866) for 1 block, then left again between the second and third houses to enter the cemetery driveway.

Gen. Jeb Stuart.

ABINGDON SW 10

This was an important railroad depot and supply base during the war. In 1862 townspeople contributed all of the church bells to the Confederacy, to be melted for casting cannon. At different times, Confederate Gens. John Hunt Morgan and John C. Breckinridge used Abingdon as headquarters. Joseph E. John-

Martha Washington Inn, Abingdon.

ston grew up and attended school in the town, while John S. Mosby mustered into the Southern ranks there in 1861.

Federal troops captured the town in December 1864 and set fire to a number of the main dwellings.

MARTHA WASHINGTON INN

Still in use as a hotel, and little altered from its Civil War appearance, this large inn served as a military hospital for much of the conflict.

Located on the south side of Main Street, directly across from the world-famous Barter Theater.

SINKING SPRING CEMETERY

This cemetery boasts several Civil War–era connections, including a walled-in area containing a large tombstone to "Unknown Confederate Dead." The exact number of Southern soldiers buried here is not known. However, the burial plot originated in September 1861 when 17 Louisiana soldiers were killed in a train wreck on the edge of town. Sinking Springs is also the final resting place for former Virginia governor, secretary of war, and Confederate Gen. John B. Floyd.

One block north of W. Main Street on Alternate U.S. 58 West.

WISE   SW 11

Known as Gladeville at the time of the Civil War, Wise served for
a time in 1862 as the headquarters for Confederate Gen. Humphrey Marshall. Subsequently, the citizens of Wise suffered multiple Union raids, including a skirmish on July 7, 1863, that left
their village in ruins.

POUND GAP   SW 12

One of the few avenues through the rugged mountains of ex-
treme southwestern Virginia, this spot was the scene of two
skirmishes and two brisk engagements fought for control of the
pass. Future president James A. Garfield commanded Federal
troops in one of the actions. In December 1864 Union forces
permanently secured the gap. Vestiges of earthworks are said to
exist in the woods on either side of the mountain pass.

Located on U.S. 23 at the Virginia–Kentucky border.

CRANESNEST   SW 13

The Unionist sentiments of a family who ran a grist mill located
here prompted occasional attention from local Southern troops,
but the most significant action came when a force of approximately 200 to 400 members of the 7th Battalion Confederate
Cavalry clashed with 70 Federal "home guards" here on November 9, 1864. The Unionists fled, leaving 8 to 10 of their number
who were killed in the brief firefight that symbolized the type of
engagements common to the region.

*A stone marker is located on Virginia 72 North just across the
Dickinson County line from Wise, 11.6 miles from Coeburn.*

JONESVILLE   SW 14

The Lee County seat was the scene of several skirmishes between
Union and Confederate forces in 1863 and 1864. The largest
of these engagements came in January 1864, when Brig. Gen.

Gen. Burnside's Army Occupying Cumberland Gap, from *Harper's Weekly,* 1863.

William E. ("Grumble") Jones defeated and captured a contingent of the 16th Illinois Cavalry.

CUMBERLAND GAP   SW 15

Six times during the war, opposing forces skirmished over possession of this vital gateway between the Eastern and Western theaters of the war. Today, a roadside historical marker calls attention to Cumberland Gap's Civil War history. A dazzling view from its heights offers moving proof of this site's strategic importance during the sectional conflict. Known popularly during the war as the "Gibraltar" of America, Cumberland Gap is a National Historical Park in the National Park Service system.

Cumberland Gap is on U.S. 58 at the Virginia–Kentucky–Tennessee border. Area sites also include the Wilderness Road State Park in Virginia and the Abraham Lincoln Museum at Lincoln Memorial University in Harrogate, Tennessee.

Specialized Tour Suggestions

It should be noted at the outset that following these events in a strict chronological order based on the war's timeline will likely not be cost-effective for the traveler. You may choose instead to tour sites whose dates cross from earlier to later in the conflict, recognizing that the Civil War often took different turns over the same ground.

OPENING SALVOS

Travel from Norfolk (SE 15, p. 75) and Portsmouth (SE 16, p. 76) to Forts Monroe and Wool (SE 14, pp. 73–75). The June 10, 1861, engagement of Big Bethel is also in the Hampton region (SE 14, p. 73). Travel north to Alexandria (NE 1, p. 33) and Arlington (NE 2, p. 37), then on to the site of the first major battle of the war, First Manassas (or First Bull Run; NE 5, p. 42). The small but sharp fight at Ball's Bluff occurred on October 21, 1861, near Leesburg (NC 1, p. 19). These locations represent the earliest operations of the Civil War in Virginia.

CONFEDERATE CAPITALS

Richmond (SE 3, p. 55) offers extensive Civil War–related sites, including the White House of the Confederacy and the Museum of the Confederacy. The last capital can be found at Danville (SC 11, p. 97).

ROBERT E. LEE

While General Lee is obviously associated with multiple military campaigns and engagements in Virginia, he also has connections to various residences and non-battle sites.

Alexandria (NE 1, p. 37) was the location of his boyhood home and Arlington (NE 2, pp. 37–38) the site of the Custis-Lee Mansion now incorporated in Arlington Cemetery. Stratford Hall (NE 6, p. 43) was Lee's birthplace. The Stewart-Lee House in Richmond (SE 3, p. 60) served as his wartime residence in the capital. Derwent (SC 2, p. 90) served as a refuge for Lee's family during the war and as a temporary home for the general after it. Turnbull House and Violet Bank were his headquarters in Petersburg (SE 20, pp. 82–83). Lexington (NW 16, p. 17) was the general's last home while he served as president of Washington College, and his final resting place is in Lee Memorial Chapel at Washington and Lee University there.

Other significant sites include Fort Monroe (SE 14, pp. 73–74) where Lee was stationed before the Civil War for a time. Additional Lee connections can be found in Bath County (NW 14, Warm Springs, p. 14), Orange (NC 13, Saint Thomas's Episcopal Church, pp. 27–28), and Shirley Plantation in Charles City County (SE 7, pp. 65–66).

NAVAL/RIVER WAR

Begin at Norfolk (SE 15, p. 75) or Portsmouth (SE 16, p. 76) as the neighboring cities were both important to naval affairs in Tidewater Virginia. Be sure to visit the Hampton Roads Naval Museum at Nauticus in downtown Norfolk. Proceed to Forts Monroe and Wool (SE 14, pp. 73–75) and be sure to make sufficient time for the Mariners' Museum (SE 13, p. 71). From Newport News, cross the James River on Highway 17 and follow Route 10 to Smithfield to visit Forts Boykin and Huger (SE 18, pp. 78–79). A side trip to Suffolk (SE 17, p. 78) will enable you to visit the area of the Nansemond River defenses there. Be sure to include Drewry's Bluff (Fort Darling; SE 5, p. 63) off I-95 south of Richmond.

1862 PENINSULA CAMPAIGN

For a sense of the full extent of this campaign begin at Fort Monroe (SE 14, pp. 73–74), then cross to Hampton and Newport News (SE 13, p. 70) on the Virginia Peninsula. A visit to Yorktown (SE 12, p. 68) will highlight the positions where George McClellan got bogged down by John Magruder in the earliest phases of the campaign. The opposing forces fought a bitter rear-guard action in driving rain at Williamsburg (SE 8, p. 66) and proceeded to the vicinity of the Confederate capital (SE 3, pp. 55–56) where the battle of Seven Pines or Fair Oaks occurred. With Joseph Johnston's wounding and Robert E. Lee's ascendency to command, the rest of the campaign comprised the Seven Days' battles on what were then the outskirts of Richmond, beginning with the battle of Mechanicsville and ending at Malvern Hill. In the course of the operation McClellan shifted his headquarters to the James River.

SHENANDOAH VALLEY, 1862 AND 1864

This picturesque area of the commonwealth experienced war in multiple phases, most prominently in 1862 during Stonewall Jackson's Valley campaign and the 1864 advances of Philip Sheridan. Numerous raids and smaller operations dotted the region as well.

For sites associated with Jackson and his "Foot Cavalry," be sure to visit Winchester (NW 1, p. 4), Cross Keys (NW 11, pp. 11–12), Port Republic (NW 12, p. 12), and McDowell (NW 13, pp. 12–13). "Circle Tour" and Civil War Trails markers will prove invaluable through much of this region.

Areas connected to Sheridan's actions in 1864 include Winchester (NW 1, p. 4), Cedar Creek (NW 2, pp. 6–7), Fisher's Hill near Strasburg (NW 4, pp. 8–9), Edinburg (NW 5, p. 9), and Waynesboro (NW 15, p. 15). Sites outside of the Shenandoah Valley that also have connections to Sheridan are Trevilian Station (NC 16, p. 30), Yellow Tavern (SE 2, p. 54), Five Forks and Burnt Quarter in Dinwiddie County (SE 22, p. 84), and Amherst (SC 8, p. 94).

MOSBY'S CONFEDERACY

Sites associated with the famed Southern partisan are found at Leesburg (NC 1, p. 19), Warrenton (NC 5, p. 22–23), Fairfax County (NE 3, p. 39), and Front Royal (NW 3, p. 8). Areas outside "Mosby's Confederacy" that are of significance include Old Glade Spring Presbyterian Cemetery (SW 8, p. 102) and Abingdon (SW 10, pp. 103–4).

JEB STUART'S CAVALRY

The most flamboyant of Confederate horsemen, Jeb Stuart served as the "Eyes of Lee's Army." Of particular importance are Hanover County (SE 1, p. 53), Yellow Tavern (SE 2, p. 54), Kelly's Ford (NC 7, pp. 23–24), Brandy Station (NC 8, pp. 24–25), Culpeper and the History Museum (NC 9, p. 25), and Trevilian Station (NC 16, p. 30); other areas linked to Stuart include Alexandria (NE 1, pp. 34, 36), Lynchburg (SC 9, p. 94), and Emory (SW 9, p. 103).

ADDITIONAL CAVALRY OPERATIONS

Key sites include the "Beefsteak Raid" (SE 19 and SE 23, pp. 80 and 84–85), Christiansburg (SW 3, p. 100), Wytheville (SW 5, p. 100), Marion (SW 6, p. 101), Goochland County (NC 17, p. 31), Waterford (NC 2, p. 21), Aldie (NC 3, p. 21), Warrenton (NC 5, p. 22), and Little Fork Church (NC 6, p. 23).

HOSPITALS AND MEDICINE

Although few structures escaped being used as makeshift hospital facilities when engagements occurred nearby, a number of museums and Civil War sites explore the role of the medical profession during and in the immediate aftermath of the conflict. Chimborazo Medical Museum in Richmond (SE 3, p. 58) is a must for the visitor interested in this aspect of Civil War history. The Civil War Museum at the Exchange Hotel in Gordonsville (NC 14, pp. 28–29) also features medical displays, while Winchester (NW 1, pp. 4,6), Warrenton (NC 5, p. 22), Culpeper (NC 9, p. 25), Charlottesville (NC 15, p. 29), Lynchburg (SC 9, p. 94), and Bedford (SC 10, p. 96) had numerous hospitals.

AFRICAN AMERICAN EXPERIENCE

The African American experience in the Civil War reflects the transitional status of slaves to freedmen and -women. Hampton (SE 14, pp. 73–74) is the place where Union Gen. Benjamin Butler first used the term "contraband" to refer to slaves and others of African descent who sought refuge in his lines, and Suffolk (SE 17, p. 76) held a large "Contraband Camp." Alexandria (NE 1, pp. 34–35) contains several sites including the Freedmen's Cemetery and Freedom House Museum, while a hospital in the

Exchange Hotel in Gordonsville (NC 14, pp. 28–29) served the Freedmen's Bureau.

Of the sites where African American soldiers served during the war, the best known stem from the siege of Petersburg and operations outside Richmond in 1864. Be sure to visit the National Park Headquarters at Tredegar Ironworks in Richmond (SE 3, p. 56) and Fort Harrison (SE 2, p. 55). On the Petersburg National Battlefield a trip to the Crater (SE 20, p. 81) is a must. A smaller engagement that featured United States Colored Troops occurred at Wilson's Wharf in Charles City County (SE 7, p. 64). See also the Gardner Monument in Gloucester County (SE 11, p. 67), and Saltville (SW 7, pp. 101–2).

1864 OVERLAND CAMPAIGN

Ulysses S. Grant's operations began with action at the Wilderness (NE 8, pp. 47–48) and continued to Spotsylvania Courthouse (NE 9, p. 48). Massaponax Church (NE 10, p. 49) is another significant site associated with General Grant. Follow this action through the area of the North Anna Battlefield (NE 14, p. 51) to Cold Harbor (SE 3, p. 57) and cross the James River to trace where the Army of the Potomac engaged the Confederates at Petersburg (SE 20, pp. 80–82). A side trip will enable you to survey the fighting between Richmond and Petersburg associated with the Army of the James and Gen. Benjamin Butler, (SE 4, pp. 62–63).

WAR ON THE SOUTHWEST BORDERLANDS

To view areas of this region that forces in Blue and Gray contested visit Cloyd's Mountain outside Dublin (SW 4, p. 100), Saltville (SW 7, pp. 101–2), Wise (SW 11, p. 105), Pound Gap (SW 12, p. 105), Jonesville (SW 14, pp. 105–6), and Cumberland Gap (SW 15, p. 106). Recall that geographical constraints through much of the region prevented substantial troop movements, but that the area was susceptible to raids.

APPOMATTOX CAMPAIGN

Begin at Petersburg National Battlefield (SE 20, p. 81). Pamplin Historical Park (SE 22, pp. 83–84) is on the site of a portion of the breakthrough that followed. Proceed to Five Forks in

Dinwiddie County (SE 22, p. 84), the scene of actions that saw the sudden end of the lengthy siege of Petersburg. Next travel to Amelia (SC 3, p. 90) and follow the retreat of Robert E. Lee's haggard Army of Northern Virginia to Sailor's Creek (SC 4, pp. 90–91), then on to Appomattox Courthouse (SC 7, pp. 92–94).

Index

Illustration Credits